—— Step-by-Step ——
WOODEN
TOYS

Step-by-Step

WOODEN TOYS

ROGER HORWOOD

PHOTOGRAPHY BY JUAN ESPI

ILLUSTRATIONS BY CLARENCE CLARKE

STACKPOLE
BOOKS

Published by
STACKPOLE BOOKS
5067 Ritter Road
Mechanicsburg, PA 17055

Printed in Malaysia by Times Offset (M) Sdn Bhd

10 9 8 7 6 5 4 3 2 1

Originally published in the U.K. in 1993 by New Holland (Publishers) Ltd.

Editor: Elizabeth Frost
Designer: Janice Evans
Assistant designer: Lellyn Creamer
Photographer: Juan Espi
Typeset by Diatype Setting
Reproduction by Unifoto (Pty) Ltd

Library of Congress Cataloging-in-Publication Data
 Horwood, Roger.
     Step-by-step wooden toys / Roger Horwood:
photography by Juan Espi: illustrations by Clarence Clarke.
         p. cm.
     Includes bibliographical references (p.)
     ISBN 0-8117-2936-2
     1. Wooden toy making.   I. Title.
 TT174.5.W6H67   1997
 745. 592—dc20   96-18664
                                              CIP

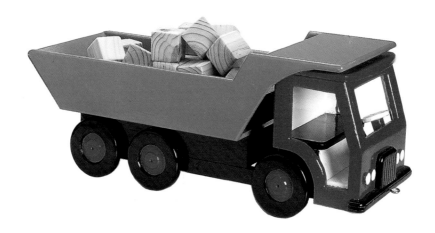

CONTENTS

INTRODUCTION

In recent years there has been a worldwide resurgence of interest in natural materials such as wood. Not surprisingly, wooden toys have gained popularity too.

The purpose of this book is to help you make beautiful wooden toys that will delight children and bring you, the woodworker, an enormous amount of pleasure and satisfaction. The instructions—from the type and size of wood to buy, to the step-by-step details of cutting out and construction — are designed to make the job as simple and straightforward as possible. Projects range in complexity from easy (skill level 1) to advanced (skill level 3), so you can begin on a level that you are comfortable with and progress to more challenging work.

Though many of the projects are directed at the beginner, it is beyond the scope of this book to offer a complete course in basic woodworking. General information on selecting wood, buying tools and preparing the wood for projects is provided in the next few pages, but it may be necessary to consult a reliable textbook on woodwork techniques or an experienced woodworker when trying a technique for the first time, particularly if you will be using tools with which you are unfamiliar.

If you've never worked with wood before and find the prospect daunting, be encouraged by the fact that people of both sexes and all levels of ability achieve excellent results and derive enormous pleasure from this engrossing pastime. Once you have attained the basic skills of woodworking, and have tried a few of the simple designs in this book, then the sky's the limit — you can design your own, or copy other designs and produce toys of a really fine quality that will bring you a very satisfying sense of achievement.

TYPES OF WOOD

The woods used for toymaking are generally inexpensive in comparison to the imported and special hardwoods used in furniture making, and a few easily obtainable woods will do the job for almost all toymaking projects.

Pine This is a soft wood, generally a clean white colour, which is easy and pleasant to work and in plentiful supply. The timber industry has come up with a very practical method of making boards of a reasonable size and uniform quality. Called 'copine', these boards are made of strips of pine approximately 20 mm (¾ in) wide, which are glued together under pressure. Using this simple method, good boards of almost any width and length can be produced. These boards can be purchased from most local hardware stores in a great variety of widths and lengths. This is very good toymaking material.

Medium density fibre or MDF board This is manufactured by a process of reducing wood to a very fine fibre, mixing it with a resin and then compressing it under pressure to form sheets. Standard sizes and thicknesses vary from country to country, 12 mm (½ in), or the closest available thickness, being the most suitable for toymaking on our sort of scale. Your local hardware store or wood yard should be able to supply sheets of almost any size you require.

Plywood This is made by laminating thin sheets of wood so that the grain of each sheet is at right angles to the one adjacent to it (diagram 1).

DIAGRAM 1

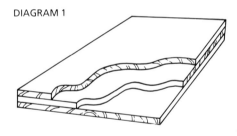

Plywood is usually made in sheets of 2440 mm x 1220 mm (8 ft x 4 ft) and in a variety of thicknesses, ranging from a very thin 3 ply of about 3 mm (⅛ in) to multi-plys of about 25 mm (1 in). Again, your local wood yard will probably supply just about any dimensions you require.

Plywood is very good for toymaking as it is strong and has a uniform thickness throughout, and can be cut into almost any shape and still retain its strength.

Getting the feel of wood

One of the joys of working with wood is the wonderful feel and smell of the various timbers. A good way to become familiar with the types and sizes of wood available for toymaking is to go to a wood yard and wander around with a notebook and ruler. Look at the wood, feel it, handle it, smell it and make notes. The dealer should be sympathetic to your growing knowledge of the subject and will be very happy to advise you, particularly if you're likely to become a regular customer!

TOOLS OF THE TRADE

Very good work can be achieved with just a few basic tools. It wasn't long after I arrived in South Africa in the late 1960s, having left all my tools in England, that the urge to work with wood took hold of me again! With very little money at my disposal, I bought a tenon saw, a 1" and a ½" chisel, a square, a plane, a mallet and a hammer, and with these seven basic tools I was able to produce some good, if relatively small, pieces of furniture.

The photograph on pages 8 & 9 shows a basic set of hand tools, which includes the seven mentioned above. If money is a problem, buy the essentials first and then gradually build up your tool set, but try to follow the maxim, 'Buy good — buy once'. A good quality, if somewhat expensive, tool will literally last you a lifetime if cared for, whereas a poor quality tool will probably not do the job effectively and may break in a short time, forcing you to buy again.

A good tool becomes a part of you as you use it. You become familiar with its weight, its feel and the way it looks, and it becomes such a friend that if you leave it unused in your workshop for too long it becomes lonely and may sulk the next time you try to use it — this may account for the fact that the quality of your work sometimes slips if you are out of the workshop for too long!

Care of tools

In a warm, dry climate tools will last for a long time if they are stored and protected. Tools should always be stored separately from one another in boxes or on racks. Don't throw them together in a heap or a box, as the cutting edges will damage one another. Protect cutting edges by laying tools carefully on the work surface. Lay planes on their side and not on their face, as anything hard will 'gap' the blade.

If you live in a damp or humid climate, give all the metal parts of your tools a very gentle rub over with a light oil and store them in cupboards or boxes, as far away from damp as possible. If your tools still sustain rust patches, a light sanding with emery cloth followed by a little more oil will usually solve the problem.

CROSS-CUT SAW (PANEL SAW)

TENON SAW

KEYHOLE SAW

RETRACTABLE STEEL TAPE MEASURE

DOVETAIL SAW

BRADAWL

GIMLET

COPING SAW

BEVEL-EDGE CHISELS

SURFORM RASP

FIRMER CHISEL

JACK PLANE

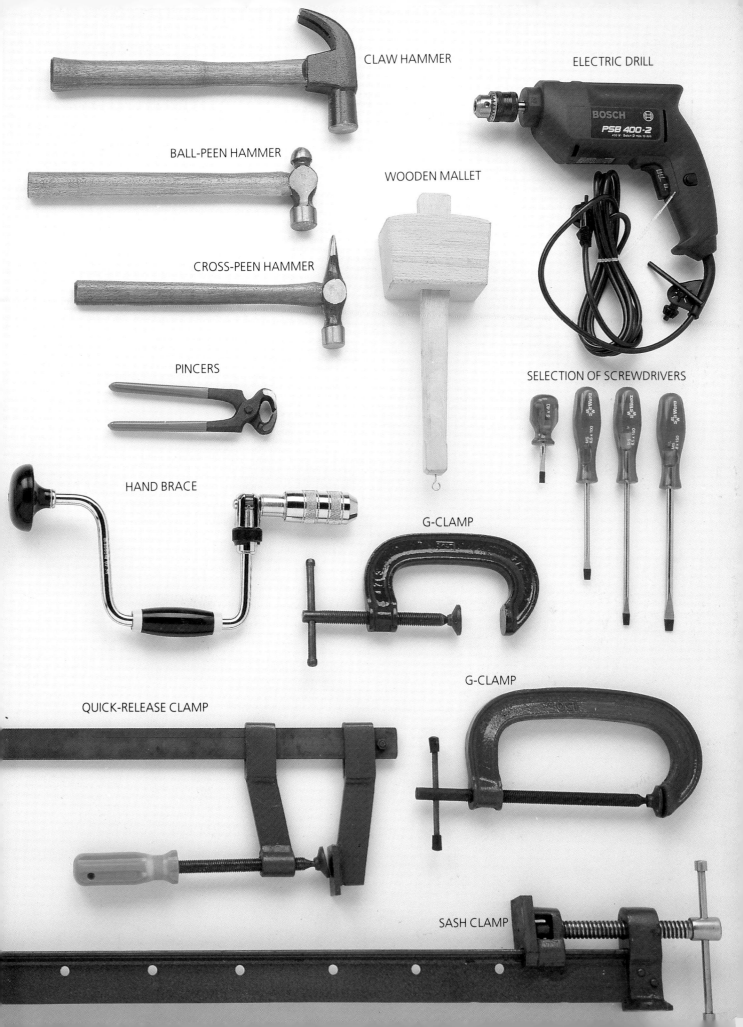

CLAW HAMMER

ELECTRIC DRILL

BALL-PEEN HAMMER

WOODEN MALLET

CROSS-PEEN HAMMER

PINCERS

SELECTION OF SCREWDRIVERS

HAND BRACE

G-CLAMP

G-CLAMP

QUICK-RELEASE CLAMP

SASH CLAMP

Sharpening tools

Sharpening saw blades is best left to the professionals! Ask your local hardware store to recommend a good saw sharpener.

Some care and practice is necessary to get a good cutting edge on cutting blades such as chisels and blades. Two angles are involved — the grinding angle of 30°, and the cutting angle of 45° (diagram 2).

DIAGRAM 2

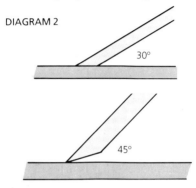

The grinding angle is best achieved on a slow-moving, water-lubricated sandstone, but most hobbyists do not have access to such luxuries. With a little practice the same result can be achieved using a coarse stone or an electric grindstone, provided that the tool is handled very carefully and kept constantly cool by dipping it in lubricating oil or a bowl of water. If the blade is not kept cool in this way, it will overheat, the edge will turn blue, and it will lose its temper (that is, the quality of the steel will deteriorate — it won't have a tantrum!).

Once the grinding edge has been established and the blade is square, then the cutting angle is established by a light application on a flat grindstone. Sand just the tip of the blade to 45°; once the blade becomes blunt with use, the cutting angle can be re-established with the gentle use of the flat grindstone lubricated with oil (diagram 3).

It is possible to buy a chisel sharpening guide, into which blades can be clamped so that when they are sharpened, a perfect angle of 45° is achieved. Your local hardware store will be able to help you with this.

DIAGRAM 3

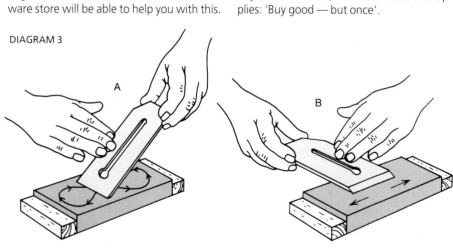

MACHINERY

Electrical machinery has made the job of the woodworker considerably easier. The advantage of machines is that they generally do the work much faster (and sometimes more accurately) than the woodworker, but there are several disadvantages, such as the noise they produce, the storage space they require, the potential danger involved in their use, and their cost.

Noise Electrical woodworking machines tend to be very noisy, and as most hobbyists work at home, consideration must be given to neighbours. The use of noisy tools at inconvenient times, such as late at night and on Sunday afternoons, will do nothing for your popularity in the neighbourhood!

Space Machines are generally much larger than the hand tools for which they are the substitutes, and it is important that there is enough working space around them. Because of this, you may find machinery impractical, or that your car spends more time in the street than in the garage!

Danger Most woodworking machines function on the principle of a very sharp cutting edge or surface rotating at high speed, with the wood held and guided by hand. This makes woodworking machinery among the most dangerous used. EXTREME CAUTION must be exercised at all times when using this type of machinery. Carelessness has resulted in some horrific accidents, ranging from loss of fingers to loss of life.

Protective equipment is essential — goggles for the eyes, dust masks for protection of the lungs and ear muffs for the prevention of damage to hearing.

Cost Woodworking machinery is much more expensive than hand tools are, and the more sophisticated the tool, the more it will cost you. However, if you do decide to buy electrical tools, the same basic rule applies: 'Buy good — but once'.

A good electric drill is one very basic electrical tool that will always be worthwhile. An amazing variety of attachments is available to the hobbyist. Generally, these attachments aren't suitable for heavy and sustained use, but for the home workshop they are usually excellent.

JOINING WOOD

Most of the joints used to make the projects in this book are simple butt joints. This simply means that the two pieces of wood that are to be joined together are 'butted' up to each other and fixed together, usually with glue and a screw.

Glue There are several good wood glues on the market and your local hardware store will be able to advise you on the pros and cons of the various brands. Worth mentioning here is the fact that the most popular 'white' wood glues perform very well indeed as long as they are not exposed to wet conditions. Therefore, for toys that are likely to spend much of their lives in the rain, a waterproof wood glue is advisable.

Screws Again, there are several varieties on the market, but for toymaking purposes, steel screws — or more attractive brass screws — with countersunk heads will be perfectly adequate (see photograph below).

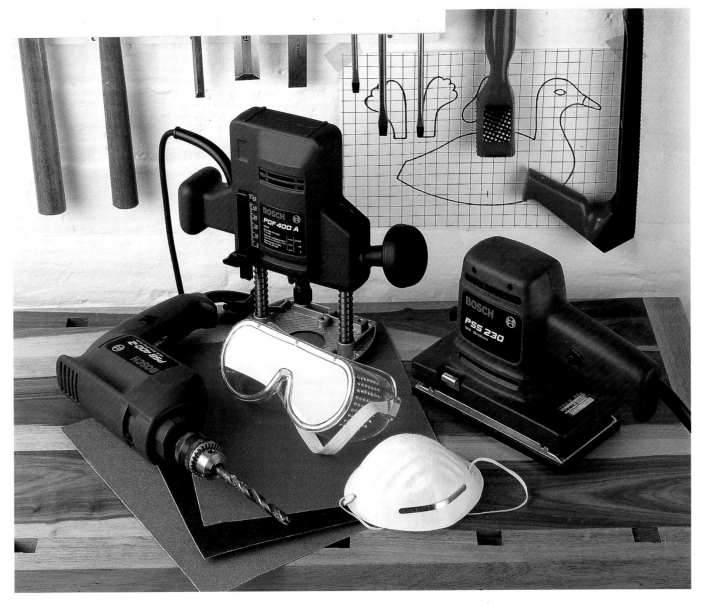

It is a good idea to know the names of the screws you will be using. Usually, two measurements are used: i) the length and ii) the thickness, which is given as a number — the lower the number, the thinner the screw. So, if you ask for 'Two dozen, 30 mm, number 8, steel countersunk head screws', the shop assistant will know exactly what you want. The '30' refers to the length of the screw in millimetres and the 'number 8' refers to the size, which in this case is a good general-purpose screw.

Always screw from the thinner wood into the thicker wood. The way the wood is being joined in diagram 4(a) is incorrect and will end in disaster, whereas diagram 4(b) is correct and will result in a strong join.

A close look at diagram 4(c) will reveal that three operations are necessary to secure the screw:

i) drill a hole through the wood marked A, wide enough to allow the chosen screw free access through the wood;

ii) countersink this hole with a countersink bit so that the head of the screw will be about 3 mm (⅛ in) below the surface of the wood. This will allow you to fill the hole with wood filler at a later stage to create an uninterrupted surface for painting;

iii) drill a lead hole into the wood marked B. This hole will be the same width as the shank of the screw and as long as the depth to which the screw is going to penetrate into the wood.

DIAGRAM 4a

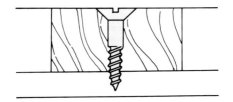

DIAGRAM 4b

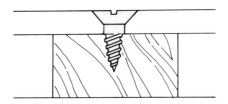

DIAGRAM 4c

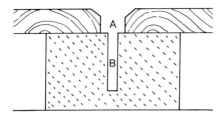

PREPARING FOR YOUR PROJECT

Many, many excellent books have been written on the subject of woodworking and, like every other subject requiring any level of learning and skill, the more you read and learn, the better.

Look at books on woods, tools and techniques and spend a little money on a few reliable reference works that will improve your knowledge and skill.

The following few introductory hints and comments will give you a good start, but you will never stop learning and improving!

Rules you just don't break

Here are just a few basic rules that will help you to produce good results.

Never rush a job Working with wood and making wooden toys is a very enjoyable hobby. One golden rule to remember is that the faster you try to do the job, the more mistakes you're likely to make.

This means planning well in advance and planning carefully. If you try working to a tight deadline, you are likely to make a basic mistake that will eventually cost you more time and money. Take your time, measure carefully, cut carefully, and finish off carefully. Enjoy your time in the workshop and you will derive an enormous amount of fulfilment and satisfaction. After 35 years of working with wood, I can assure you that this is at the top of the list of rules you just don't break!

Measure twice; cut once It's not difficult to rectify a mistake made when measuring for a cut, but when you cut to a wrong measurement and find that your lovely piece of wood is the wrong size, the frustration and probable waste involved can be very upsetting.

One way to prevent this is to take your measurement and make a pencil mark at this spot. Take your tape measure away, check that you have read the measurement on the plan correctly and then measure the same piece from the other direction. If the two measurements and the plan check out, then it should be safe to go ahead and cut. Follow this simple rule, and frustration will be kept to a minimum.

Marking face sides and edges

Most of the wood you'll buy for making the toys in this book will be ready to work with. In other words, all the surfaces will be clean and flat, the corners will be square and the sides or edges will be square to the surfaces.

However, some wood may need work before it is ready to use. Pine boards, for example, may fall into this category. In this case, follow the steps below:

Face side This is the surface that will be visible. Choose the best-looking one, making sure it is flat and smooth; make a face side mark on this surface (diagram 5).

DIAGRAM 5

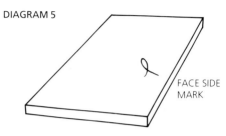

FACE SIDE MARK

Face edge Lay your set square with the stock on the face edge and see if the edge is square. Run the square along the whole edge and put a pencil mark at every place where it is not exactly square (diagram 6).

DIAGRAM 6

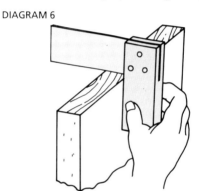

Plane the edge until it is straight and true and square; make a face edge mark on the edge touching the face side (diagram 7).

DIAGRAM 7

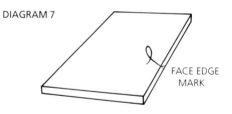

FACE EDGE MARK

Now that this surface and edge are square and true, all your measurements can be made using these as reference points.

Square ends from the face edge Lay your square as close to the chosen end as possible, and making sure that the stock of the square is firmly against the face edge, draw a line across the face side (diagram 8).

DIAGRAM 8

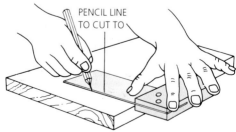

PENCIL LINE TO CUT TO

Important When drawing a line against an edge, make sure that your pencil point is sharp and angle it so that the line drawn is as close as possible to the edge. This will give you an accurate line (diagram 9).

DIAGRAM 9

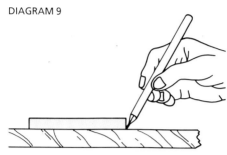

Reverse the square and drop a pencil line down the face edge. Repeat the process on the other side (diagram 10).

DIAGRAM 10

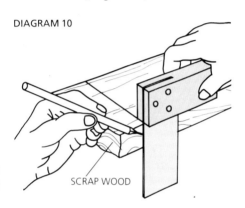

SCRAP WOOD

You will have drawn lines for a true and square end that can now be sawn.

Saw and chisel cuts The line you make on a piece of wood indicates the exact position of the cut you want to make. Therefore, always cut or chisel on the *scrap side of the line*. If you cut on the line you will be cutting into the measured part and the end result will be inaccurate (diagram 11).

DIAGRAM 11

GROOVE CREATED BY SAW CUT

Paint When finishing toys, always use a non-toxic paint.

Now select a project — and have a go! Don't be afraid to try challenging projects — learn from your mistakes and don't repeat them. Good luck and enjoy yourself!

WADDLING DUCK

This traditional waddling duck makes a delightful gift for a toddler. Keep the finished design simple or paint your duck in a selection of bright colours.

SKILL LEVEL 1

Materials

1 x 300 mm x 230 mm x 22 mm
(12 in x 9 in x ⅞ in) piece pine
1 x 120 mm x 60 mm (4¾ in x 2½ in)
piece hardboard OR
4 mm (⅛ in) plywood
1 x 750 mm x 14 mm (2 ft 4 in x ½ in)
dowel rod
1 old rubber car inner tube OR
a piece of thin leather
Sandpaper
Stapler OR
upholstery tacks
Wax candle
Wood glue
White universal undercoat
Topcoat paint

Duck

1. Enlarge the duck outline (diagram 1) to 300 mm (12 in) from tail-tip to beak-tip, using graph paper or a photocopier.

2. Place a sheet of carbon paper and the duck outline on the pine, as close as possible to one end and the bottom edge of the board and secure with drawing pins to ensure that it doesn't slip.

3. With a pencil, carefully follow the outline of the duck and the handle so that these two shapes are transferred on to the wood. Also mark the wheel-axle point (W) on the drawing so that this, too, is transferred to the wood.

4. Remove the papers and cut out the shape of the duck and the handle, using either a jig saw, a coping saw or a band saw.

5. Smooth all the outside edges and gently round off all the corners with a rasp or coarse sandpaper. Use a rasp to shape the beak so that it looks realistic from the top.

Wheels

6. Set your compass to a radius of 50 mm (2 in) and draw two circles on the remaining pine, ensuring that the centre point on each is visible. Cut out the wheels using whichever saw you used for the duck, and, with a rasp and sandpaper, smooth the flat surfaces and round the corners.

7. Using a 16 mm (¾ in) drill bit, drill through your duck at the point marked W. Put the dowel rod through this hole to ensure that it fits, yet will rotate freely.

8. Using a 14 mm (½ in) drill bit, drill a hole — off centre — in each wheel. Make sure that the circumference of the drill bit just touches the centre point of the circle (diagram 2). This hole should be drilled to only half the thickness of the wood. These holes will give the duck its 'waddle'.

DIAGRAM 1

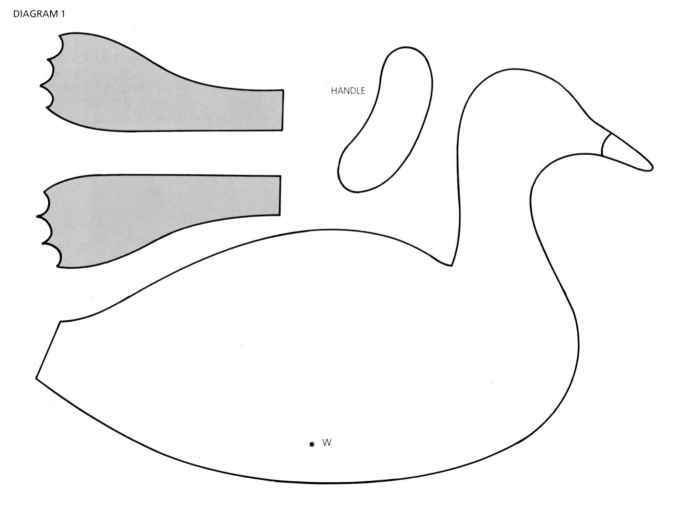

HANDLE

W

DIAGRAM 2

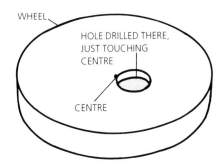

WHEEL

HOLE DRILLED THERE, JUST TOUCHING CENTRE

CENTRE

9. On each wheel, draw a line from the centre of the hole just drilled to the edge of the wheel *closest to the hole*.

DIAGRAM 3

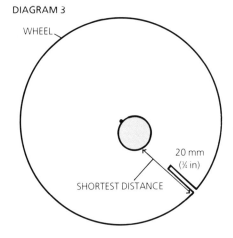

WHEEL

20 mm (¾ in)

SHORTEST DISTANCE

10. Secure each wheel in your bench vice and make a 20 mm (¾ in) cut down this line, towards the centre of the wheel (diagram 3).

Spacers

11. Set the compass to 25 mm (1 in) and draw two circles on the hardboard or plywood. Drill a hole through the centre point of each, using the 16 mm (¾ in) drill bit. Cut out the two discs and smooth them all round (diagram 4).

DIAGRAM 4

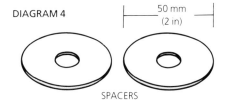

50 mm (2 in)

SPACERS

Stick and handle

12. From the dowel rod, cut a 600 mm (2 ft) length for the stick to which the handle will be attached. Cut another length of 50 mm (2 in) to use as the axle, and set aside.

13. Put the duck firmly in your bench vice, keeping the cut-off tail horizontal, and mark the centre of this section by drawing in two diagonals (diagram 5).

14. Using the smaller drill bit, drill a hole about 20 mm (¾ in) deep at this centre point, making sure that the hole is at right-angles to the surface.

15. Cut out the handle, sand it down, and round the edges.

16. Clamp the handle in your bench vice with the concave side uppermost. Repeat step 14, above, on the handle.

Feet

17. Using the feet outline provided in diagram 1, cut out two feet from the car inner tube or leather.

DIAGRAM 5

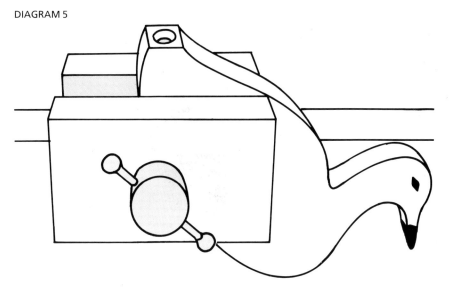

Construction and painting

18. Paint an undercoat on the wheels, stick, duck and handle. Do not paint the last 20 mm (¾ in) at each end of the stick. Do not paint the spacers or the axle.

19. When this undercoat is thoroughly dry, glue the stick firmly into the tail of the duck and the handle on to the stick. The handle should be vertical rather than horizontal. When the glue is dry, lightly rub down all the painted surfaces with a fine sandpaper to remove irregularities.

20. Paint the wheels and body with a topcoat in the colour of your choice.

21. When the paint is thoroughly dry, fit the wheels and the axle to the body of the duck *without gluing*. If there is too much 'play' between the wheels and the body, cut a couple of millimetres (½ in) off the axle and try again, until the wheels move freely but without too much 'play'.

22. Secure the feet to the wheels by inserting the thin edge of the foot into the wheel slot so that the flap sticks out *on the outside of the wheel*, that is, the side *without* the hole in it.

23. To determine the position in which the feet should be secured, hold the wheels — 'hole' sides together — with the feet at the top. Push the feet away from you, securing with a staple, or two upholstery tacks.

24. Using an ordinary household candle, give both spacers and the axle (except 10 mm [⅜ in] at each end of the axle) a good rubbing all over. This will act as a lubricant and ensure smooth running.

25. Glue one end of the axle firmly into one of the wheels. When the glue has dried, slip one of the spacers on to the axle, and slide the axle through the axle hole in the body of the duck.

26. Slip on the other spacer, dab some glue on the end of the axle, and then firmly press on the other wheel, making sure that one foot is positioned at the top and one at the bottom, as illustrated in diagram 6, and ensuring that the wheels turn smoothly, before leaving to dry.

DIAGRAM 6

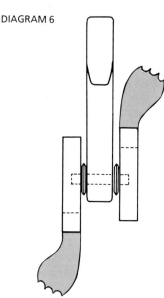

TRAIN AND CARRIAGES

This lovely toy will delight boys and girls alike. It is very adaptable, and you can make whatever number and style of parts you choose. Of course, the engine is essential, but you can do what you like with the rolling stock. I have suggested two passenger coaches and two goods carriages in addition to the engine, but you could do one of each, or three of each, or even design your own carriages using the basic format suggested in the plans as a guide.

SKILL LEVEL 2

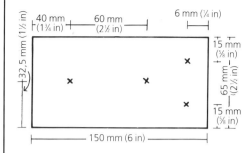
DIAGRAM 1a

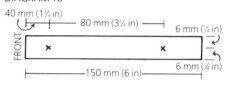
DIAGRAM 1b

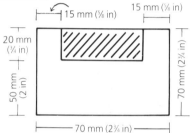
DIAGRAM 1c

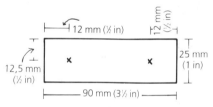
DIAGRAM 1d

Materials
1 x 1000 mm x 1000 mm x 12 mm
  (3 ft 3 in x 3 ft 3 in x ½ in) MDF board
1 x 120 mm x 50 mm x 35 mm
  (4¾ in x 2 in x 1½ in) piece pine
1 x 100 mm x 65 mm x 5 mm
  (4 in x 2½ in x ¼ in) plywood per unit
1 x 35 mm x 25 mm (1½ in x 1 in)
  dowel rod
6 x 25 mm (1 in) No. 8 countersunk steel
  screws per unit, including engine
4 x 30 mm (1¼ in) mirror screws per unit
4 x 10 mm (⅜ in) steel washers per unit
500 mm (1 ft 6 in) chain with links of
  approximately 10 mm (⅜ in)
1 small curtain wire hook and eye
  per unit
Sandpaper
Wood glue
Panel pins
Wood filler
White universal undercoat
Topcoat paint

Cab
4. For the engine cab, cut two 70 mm (2¾ in) squares from the MDF board and glue them together.

5. When dry, draw on lines for the window, as shown in diagram 1c and, using a coping saw or a band saw, cut out the scrap (indicated by hatching on the diagram).

Cab roof
6. Cut a 90 mm x 25 mm (3½ in x 1 in) rectangle from the MDF board and plane it to a thickness of 8 mm (⅜ in).

7. Drill two 4 mm (⅛ in) holes (diagram 1d), and countersink. Round off the corners and the edges with a rasp and sandpaper.

Engine
Base
1. For the base, cut a rectangle measuring 150 mm x 65 mm (6 in x 2½ in) from the MDF board. Mark the face side. This side will face upwards.

2. Drill and countersink four 4 mm (⅛ in) holes on the underside of the base as shown in diagram 1a.

3. Mark and drill two 2 mm (1/16 in) holes on each long edge of the rectangle as shown in diagram 1b. (Note that the measurements are taken from the front each time.) These holes are the lead holes for the mirror screws that will secure the wheels to the base.

Boiler

8. Cut a 115 mm x 45 mm (4½ in x 1¾ in) rectangle from the piece of pine. On one of the narrow edges, round off the two top corners as shown in diagram 4, which is a front view.

DIAGRAM 4

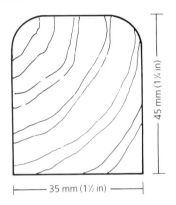

45 mm (1¾ in)

35 mm (1½ in)

Funnel

9. Cut 30 mm (1¼ in) from the dowel rod. At one end, drill a 10 mm (⅜ in) hole vertically into the wood, but only to a depth of 20 mm (¾ in). Drill through the remainder of the length of wood with a 4 mm (⅛ in) drill bit as shown in diagram 5.

DIAGRAM 5

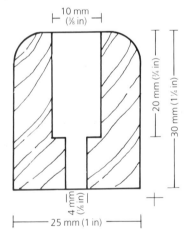

10 mm (⅜ in)

20 mm (¾ in)

30 mm (1¼ in)

4 mm (⅛ in)

25 mm (1 in)

Wheels

You will need four wheels for each unit including the engine. Multiply the number of units you're making by four and make the whole batch of wheels at the same time.

10. Using a compass, draw the required number of circles with a radius of 20 mm (¾ in) on the MDF board, ensuring that the centre of each of the circles is clearly visible. Using a coping saw or a band saw, carefully cut out the discs.

11. Drill a 4 mm (⅛ in) hole through the exact centre of each disc and countersink on one side.

12. Using a rasp and sandpaper, round off the edges and trim the wheels so that they are all exactly the same and perfectly circular.

Buffers

13. As there will be four buffers on each unit of the train, you will need the same number of buffers as there are wheels. Using a compass, draw the required number of circles with a radius of 5 mm (¼ in) on the plywood. Cut out these discs using a coping saw, and finish them off with sandpaper. **Warning!** Using electric tools on small pieces of wood can be dangerous.

Construction of engine

Before completing each stage in the following assembly, check that you are familiar with the relative positions of the pieces as shown in diagram 6.

14. First assemble the engine without using glue, ensuring that every piece is the right size and that everything fits together well. When you're satisfied that it's correct, set aside for later.

15. When all units have been put together 'dry', each unit can be taken apart one at a time and then constructed using glue.

(If you take all the units apart after they have been constructed 'dry', your workshop will be covered with parts and it will be an onerous task getting them together again!) Remember that a lead hole is drilled with a drill bit the width of the shank of the screw to be used, and to the same depth as the length of the screw that will extend into the screw hole.

16. Fix the cab to the base, ensuring that it is flush with the end of the base.

17. Fix the boiler to the base, ensuring that it fits tightly up against the cab and that it is exactly in the middle of the width of the base.

18. Fix on the roof of the cab, ensuring that the overlap is even all the way round, then fix the funnel to the boiler, 30 mm (1¼ in) from the front of the boiler and in the exact centre of the width of the boiler.

19. Using mirror screws (because they have attractive dome tops that are added at the end), fix the wheels to the base using the four lead holes already drilled. Make sure that there is a steel washer between the wheel and the base and that the wheel turns smoothly.

DIAGRAM 6

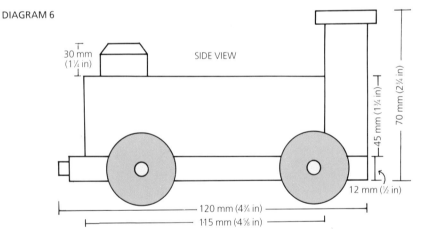

30 mm (1¼ in)

SIDE VIEW

70 mm (2¾ in)

45 mm (1¾ in)

12 mm (½ in)

120 mm (4¾ in)

115 mm (4⅝ in)

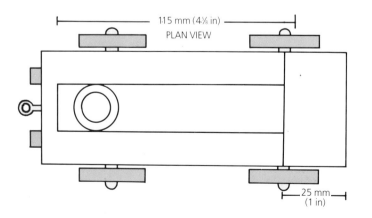

115 mm (4⅝ in)

PLAN VIEW

25 mm (1 in)

You should now have an engine that looks like the one in the photograph, except for the painting. Set aside for later.

Passenger coach
With the exception of the seat tops, all the sections for the passenger coaches are made from 12 mm (½ in) MDF board.

Base
20. Cut a 120 mm x 65 mm (4¾ in x 2½ in) rectangle and drill two 2 mm (¹⁄₁₆ in) leader holes as marked in diagram 7 (side view).

DIAGRAM 7

Ends
21. Cut two rectangles from the MDF board, each measuring 95 mm x 65 mm (3¾ in x 2½ in), and with a coping saw or band saw, cut out the rectangles for the windows, as shown in diagram 8.

22. Drill two 4 mm (⅛ in) holes in each end; countersink on one side (diagram 8).

DIAGRAM 8

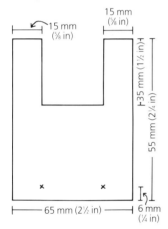

Roof
23. Cut a 160 mm x 85 mm (6¼ in x 3⅜ in) rectangle from the MDF board.

24. Drill four 4 mm (⅛ in) holes as shown in diagram 9 and countersink them on one side. Using a rasp and sandpaper, or a router, round off all four edges on the same side as the countersinking.

Seat
25. Cut two rectangles for the seat support, each 60 mm x 20 mm (2½ in x ¾ in) and two rectangles for the seat tops (from the plywood), each 65 mm x 25 mm (2½ in x 1 in). Finish off with sandpaper.

DIAGRAM 9

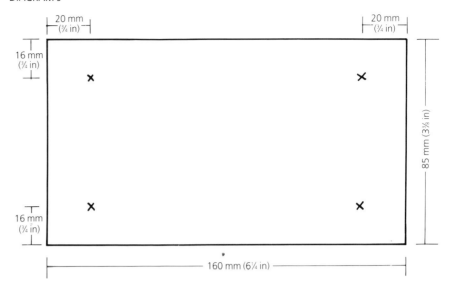

DIAGRAM 10

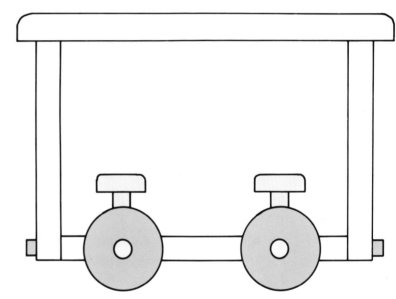

26. With a drop of glue and panel pins, fix the tops to the supports so that the support is exactly in the centre.

Construction of coach
27. Assemble the coach as shown (diagram 10). Remember to drill the lead holes for the screws. Fix the two ends to the base, ensuring that the underside is flush by clamping the base piece to the edge of your work surface, leaving enough room to add the end, and secure it in place (diagram 11).

28. Fix the seats in place as shown (diagram 10), using only glue, and allow to dry.

29. Screw the roof to the ends through the holes drilled in step 24.

DIAGRAM 11

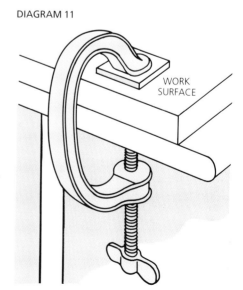

WORK SURFACE

30. Screw the wheels into position, following the instructions in step 19. You should now have a passenger coach that looks like the one in the photograph, except for the paint, buffers and couplings. Set aside for later.

Goods carriage
Base
31. Cut a rectangle measuring 120 mm x 60 mm (4¾ in x 2½ in) from the MDF board.

Ends
32. Cut two rectangles, each 65 mm x 60 mm (2½ in x 2½ in) from the MDF board.

33. Drill two 4 mm (⅛ in) holes on each piece as marked (diagram 12) and countersink the holes on one side. This will be the outside of each end.

Construction of goods carriage
35. Screw the ends to the base following the same method as for the passenger coach, above.

36. Lay the carriage on its side and fix each side in turn so that all the edges are flush.

37. Screw the wheels into position following the instructions given in step 19 above. You should now have a goods carriage that looks like the one in the photograph, except for the paint.

Assembling the engine and carriages
38. Take each unit to pieces, and reassemble one at a time, applying a thin layer of glue to each surface to be fixed together. *This excludes the wheels!*

39. Use the same method to reassemble the passenger coaches, but don't glue the roof into position until the painting has been completed, otherwise painting the interior will be quite a tricky operation!

40. When the construction is dry, finish off with sandpaper all round, then add the buffers, two at each end of each unit, as shown (diagram 14). Put a dab of glue on the inside and press firmly into position. With such small pieces of wood, it isn't really necessary to use any additional method of fixing.

Painting and finishing
41. When you are satisfied with the units, give every part a coat of white universal undercoat. When the undercoat is thoroughly dry, sandpaper smooth.

DIAGRAM 12

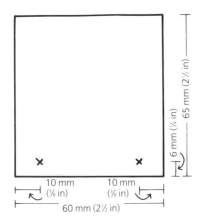

Sides
34. Cut two rectangles, 120 mm x 65 mm (4¾ in x 2½ in) from the MDF board, drill three 4 mm (⅛ in) holes on each piece as marked (diagram 13), and countersink the holes on one side. This will be the outside.

DIAGRAM 14

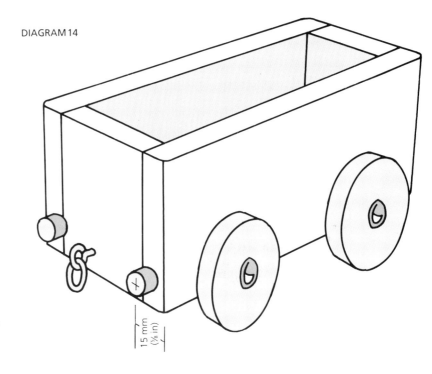

DIAGRAM 13

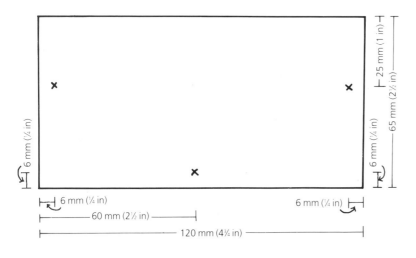

42. Apply the topcoat, either as shown in the photograph, or in the colours of your choice. It is best to use a 20 mm (¾ in) or 30 mm (1¼ in) brush for the topcoat and an artist's tipped brush for getting into the corners and for making the edges meet neatly. Don't forget that if you're putting two colours alongside each other, the first coat must be completely dry before you apply the next. Neglecting this will result in edges running into one another and paints mixing, which will spoil the final effect. You will probably need to apply two topcoats, which will be well worth the time and effort for the final effect. Remember to sand each coat lightly before applying the next.

43. When you are thoroughly satisfied with the results of your painting, attach the wheels, screwing the mirror screws just tight enough to allow each wheel to move easily without wobbling.

44. Attach the chrome domes to the tops of the mirror screws.

45. Take the chain and, using a pair of pliers, snip through each alternate link to separate the individual links, making enough to attach one to each unit. Take one of the curtain eyes, open it up about 3 mm (⅛ in) with the pliers, and slip a chain link on to it. Close up the eye so that the chain link won't come off (diagram 14).

46. In the centre of the engine base, drill a 2 mm (¹⁄₁₆ in) hole about 10 mm (⅜ in) deep and screw in a curtain eye, with the chain link attached. On the other end, screw in a curtain hook.

47. Follow the above procedure for each unit that you have made.

BOAT TO PULL

When I first made this boat 12 years ago for my son, then aged four, it was pulled all over the country — in water and out of water! Recently I asked him if I could re-paint his somewhat worse-for-wear edition for this book and he refused point blank, saying it would lose all its character. So I had to make a new one!

SKILL LEVEL 1

Materials

1 x 430 mm x 80 mm x 30 mm
   (1 ft 4 in x 3¼ in x 1¼ in) piece pine
1 x 210 mm x 45 mm x 30 mm
   (8¼ in x 1¾ in x 1¼ in) piece pine
1 x 110 mm x 45 mm x 30 mm
   (4½ in x 1¾ in x 1¼ in) piece pine
1 x 70 mm x 20 mm x 13 mm
   (2¾ in x ¾ in x ½ in) piece pine
1 x 30 mm x 25 mm (1¼ in x 1 in)
   dowel rod
4 x 35 mm (1½ in) No. 8 countersunk
   steel screws
3 x 25 mm (1 in) No. 6 countersunk
   steel screws
1 x 50 mm (2 in) No. 8 countersunk
   steel screw
1 small curtain wire eye
Sandpaper
Waterproof wood glue
Wood filler
White universal undercoat
Top coat paint

Hull

1. Mark the face edge on the top side of the 430 mm x 80 mm (1 ft 4 in x 3¼ in) rectangle of pine. Draw a centre line down the length (that is, 40 mm [1¾ in] from each edge).

2. At one end, draw an arc using a compass set at a radius of 40 mm (1¾ in). This will be the stern (back end!). On the other end, draw two lines across the hull, one 90 mm (3½ in), and the other 130 mm (5⅛ in), from the end. Join this point at each side of the hull with the end centre point (diagram 1) using a curved line drawn freehand. This will be the bow (sharp end!).

3. Using a rasp, shape both ends (diagram 2), so that they look realistic. When satisfied with the shape you have created, finish off with sandpaper and set aside.

Middle deck

4. Mark the face side on the top side of the 210 mm x 45 mm (8¼ in x 1¾ in) rectangle of pine. * Draw a line down the centre of the face side (20 mm [¾ in] from each side); continue this line vertically down one end. This end will be at the front (diagram 3).

5. Drill two 4 mm (⅛ in) thick holes through the wood as shown in diagram 3, and countersink these holes on the face side to accommodate the head of a No. 8 screw.

6. At the opposite end to the one described in the step marked * above, cut an angle of 30°. This will be at the back of the boat. To do this accurately, follow the instructions for drawing angles, which are given on page 74, step 12, diagrams 5b–5f. Finish off with sandpaper and set aside for later.

Top deck

7. Draw a line down the centre of the length of the face side of the 110 mm x 45 mm (4½ in x 1¾ in) rectangle of pine, and continue this line vertically down one end.

8. On the other end of the deck, draw the double angles (diagram 4 — plan view and diagram 5 — side view).

9. Drill two holes 4 mm (⅛ in) wide through the wood at the points marked on diagram 4 and countersink them on the face side.

DIAGRAM 1

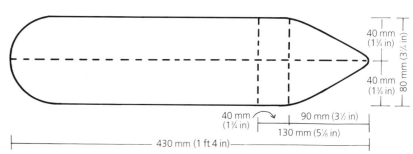

DIAGRAM 2

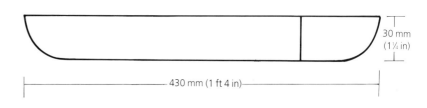

DIAGRAM 3

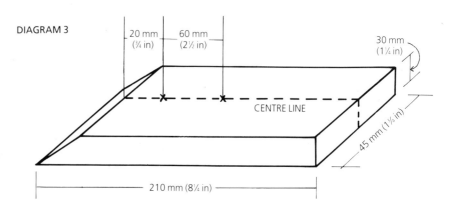

10. When you are satisfied with the angles, cut them using a tenon saw. If you have a radial-arm or bench saw, you can cut these angles by setting up your saw accordingly. Finish off with sandpaper and set aside.

DIAGRAM 4

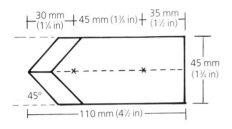

DIAGRAM 5

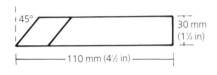

Bridge

11. Mark one of the wide surfaces of the 70 mm x 20 mm (2¾ in x ¾ in) rectangle of pine. This will be the top.

12. On the same side, draw a centre line across the top of one of the edges. This will be the front.

13. Down the length of the piece of wood, draw a centre line; this will be the guide for assembling the parts. With a 4 mm (⅛ in) drill bit, drill two holes (diagram 6) and countersink them on the face side. Finish off with sandpaper and set aside.

DIAGRAM 6

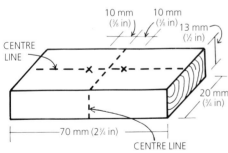

Funnel

14. Cut a 20° angle at one end of the dowel rod. This will be the end that is secured to the top deck.

15. At the other end of the dowel rod, drill a 10 mm (⅜ in) hole down the centre of the wood, *but only to a depth of 15 mm (⅝ in)* (first hole). Fix the wood vertically in the bench vice for this operation. Continue

drilling the hole that you've just drilled the rest of the way, using a 4 mm (⅛ in) drill bit (second hole). Round off the top of the dowel rod with a rasp. Finish off the piece with sandpaper and set aside (diagram 7).

DIAGRAM 7

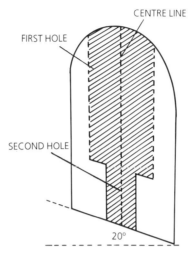

Construction

16. First assemble the boat without using glue, to make sure that everything fits together properly. It is important to

remember that when you drill a lead hole into which a screw will be set, the hole needs to be as wide as the shank of the screw, so that the wood does not split.

17. Set the top deck in position on the middle deck, with the sides and front edges flush. Drill two lead holes and, using 35 mm (1½ in) No. 8 screws, fix the top deck into position.

18. Set the bridge in position across the top deck. Drill two lead holes and, using 25 mm (1 in) No. 6 screws, fix into position (diagram 8).

19. Set this assembly in position on the top of the hull, making sure that the centre lines agree and that it is exactly in the middle of the hull. Drill two lead holes and screw the assembly to the hull using 35 mm (1½ in) No. 8 screws (diagram 8).

20. Hold the funnel in position on the top deck, making sure that it is on the centre line. Drill a lead hole and, using a 25 mm (1 in) No. 6 screw, fix into position.

21. When you're happy that the whole thing fits together well, take the vessel to pieces. Using small quantities of glue on each surface this time, reassemble the vessel as before, but do not glue the superstructure to the hull.

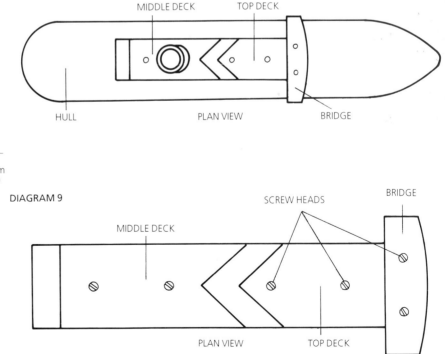

22. Fix the superstructure firmly in your bench vice and, using a rasp or a belt sander, shape a curve on the front edge as illustrated in diagram 9.

Painting

23. Paint the vessel in stages, as follows: when you're satisfied with the way the superstructure looks, glue the pieces together, and then screw the superstructure to the hull as described above.

24. Fill the screw holes with wood filler and, when the filler is thoroughly dry, sand off any excess so that the filled holes are flush with the surrounding surface.

25. Paint the whole vessel *except* the bottom with undercoat. (The reason for this may seem elementary, but you'd be surprised how many people enjoy the painting so much that they forget to leave a dry surface for the job to stand on!)

26. When the paint is dry, turn the vessel over and undercoat the bottom.

27. When dry, give the whole vessel a sanding with light sandpaper.

28. Now you're ready to paint the rest of the vessel. Remember to let each section dry thoroughly before painting another colour

next to it — and remember to do the bottom last! You might have to apply two top coats to get a really good finish, but it's worth the time and effort. Remember to sand each dry coat lightly before applying the next.

29. As no ship can do without portholes and bridge windows, these can be added with black paint, using a fine artist's brush. You may also want to add your child's initials to the funnel.

30. Finally, right on the point of the nose, drill a very small hole and screw in the curtain eye, through which a string for pulling the boat can be tied.

BLOCK BARROW

These beautiful wooden bricks have their own special barrow. Children will love being able to load and unload their cargo and can invent a variety of games to play with this versatile toy.

SKILL LEVEL 1–2

Materials
1 x 2000 mm x 55 mm x 55 mm
(6 ft 6 in x 2¼ in x 2¼ in) piece pine
1 x 670 mm x 425 mm x 22 mm (2 ft 2 in
x 1 ft 4 in x ⅞ in) piece pine
1 x 1250 mm x 45 mm x 22 mm
(4 ft 1 in x 1¾ in x ⅞ in) piece pine
1 x 50 mm x 50 mm (2 in x 2 in) piece
hardboard OR plywood
1 x 320 mm x 25 mm (12½ in x 1 in)
dowel rod OR broom handle
4 x 50 mm (2 in) No. 10 countersunk
steel screws
16 x 40 mm (1¾ in) No. 8 countersunk
steel screws
Sandpaper
Wood glue
Wood filler
Wax candle
Varnish

Blocks
1. Choose and mark the face side on the 2000 mm (6 ft 6 in) length of pine. Choose and mark the face edge, which must be exactly square to the face side. Make sure that the face side is exactly the same width as the face edge — in this case, 55 mm (2¼ in). However, it is not critical if the timber you buy is slightly thicker or thinner than this. This difference will affect the internal measurements of the barrow, but if you follow the formula in step 4, your barrow should work.

2. Cut this length of pine into pieces of the same length as the width of the wood so that you end up with 35 cubes which, if you are using wood of the specified dimensions, will be 55 mm x 55 mm x 55 mm (2¼ in x 2¼ in x 2¼ in). If working by hand, ensure that the end from which you start is square, then measure off the whole length of wood at 55 mm (2¼ in) intervals (allowing 2 mm [1⁄16 in] between the blocks for each saw cut) and square your lines all round the timber before securing to the bench and cutting (diagram 1).

DIAGRAM 1

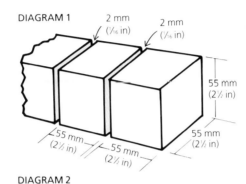

2 mm (1⁄16 in) 2 mm (1⁄16 in)
55 mm (2½ in)
55 mm (2½ in) 55 mm (2½ in) 55 mm (2½ in)

DIAGRAM 2

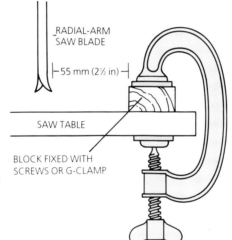

RADIAL-ARM SAW BLADE
55 mm (2½ in)
SAW TABLE
BLOCK FIXED WITH SCREWS OR G-CLAMP

DIAGRAM 3

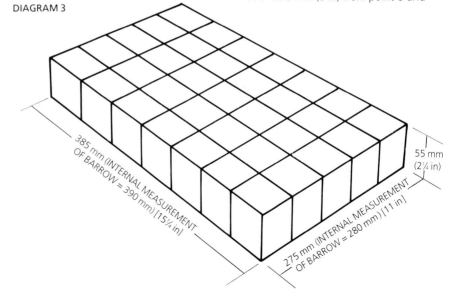

385 mm (INTERNAL MEASUREMENT OF BARROW = 390 mm) (15¼ in)
275 mm (INTERNAL MEASUREMENT OF BARROW = 280 mm) [11 in]
55 mm (2¼ in)

If using a bench saw or a radial-arm saw, mark out the first cube, and using this as a guide, fix a block of scrap wood to your saw table at the appropriate distance from the blade to ensure that all the cubes are cut to exactly the same length (diagram 2).

3. When all the cubes have been cut, sand them until each side is flat and smooth. Gently round off the corners and edges.

4. Lay the cubes on a flat surface in a 7 x 5 configuration and check the length and width of the whole configuration. If the cubes are 55 mm (2¼ in), the total size should be 385 mm x 275 mm (15¼ in x 10¾ in). If the cubes are slightly bigger or smaller, add 5 mm (¼ in) to the total length and width to establish the internal measurements of the barrow. In the case of this model, the internal measurements will be 390 mm x 280 mm (15¼ in x 11 in). The extra 5 mm (¼ in) allows some movement inside the barrow so that the cubes aren't jammed together (diagram 3).

Barrow
5. Mark out all five parts of the barrow structure on the 670 mm x 425 mm (2 ft 2 in x 1 ft 4 in) pine, allowing 2 mm (1⁄16 in) for saw cuts (see cutting plan, page 26).

6. When you have double checked and are satisfied that you have made the measurements accurately, cut out all five pieces. Keep the remaining pine for the wheels, which will be cut out later.

Side pieces
7. Choose and mark the face side and edge on each of the two side pieces. Lay the two pieces on a flat surface and mark out the exact centre of the length (point U) as shown in diagram 4. Mark two points (V), each 202 mm (8 in) from point U and

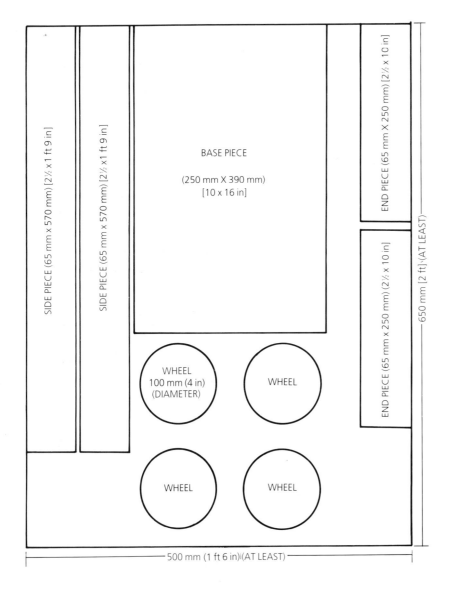

SIDE PIECE (65 mm x 570 mm) [2½ x 1 ft 9 in]

SIDE PIECE (65 mm x 570 mm) [2½ x 1 ft 9 in]

BASE PIECE

(250 mm X 390 mm)
[10 x 16 in]

END PIECE (65 mm X 250 mm) [2½ x 10 in]

END PIECE (65 mm x 250 mm) (2½ x 10 in)

650 mm [2 ft] (AT LEAST)

WHEEL
100 mm (4 in)
(DIAMETER)

WHEEL

WHEEL

WHEEL

500 mm (1 ft 6 in) (AT LEAST)

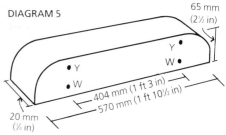

DIAGRAM 5

65 mm
(2½ in)

Y
W

Y

W

404 mm (1 ft 3 in)
570 mm (1 ft 10½ in)

20 mm
(¾ in)

End pieces

11. Mark the face side and face edge on each end piece. Hold the two pieces together to ensure that they are identical. With a marking gauge set at 5 mm (¼ in), mark both pieces along the face edges and sides (diagram 6) and pencil in.

DIAGRAM 6

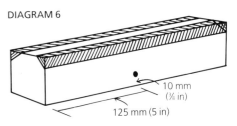

10 mm
(⅜ in)

125 mm (5 in)

12. Plane away the scrap. This creates a chamfer on each edge.

13. Mark a pencil point 10 mm (⅜ in) in from the centre point of the length on the face side of each piece so that you have two end pieces that look like diagram 7. Gently sandpaper all the edges.

DIAGRAM 7

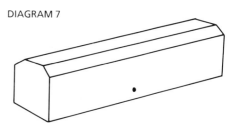

Base piece

14. If you've cut out all the pieces accurately, there's nothing else to do at this stage except to put the base aside for later!

square these two lines across. Make a strong pencil mark (point W) 15 mm (⅝ in) from each face edge, along the pencil line — these will be the axle points for the wheels.

8. Separate the two pieces and do the same as above but from the other edge (point Y).

9. On the face side of each piece, at the face edge, mark 190 mm (7½ in) from the back end of the barrow. Using a protractor, measure and mark an angle of 80° from this point so that the line will be leaning towards the back of the barrow, providing a guide for the attachment of the handle. Check that the distance between the pencil points V is 404 mm (1 ft 3 in).

10. Place the point of a compass set at a radius of 65 mm (2½ in) on point V, as close to the face edge as possible (diagram 4),

DIAGRAM 4

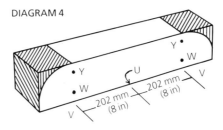

Y
W

Y

W

U

202 mm
(8 in)

202 mm
(8 in)

V

V

and draw a radius line; your two pieces should now look like diagram 4. Cut away the scrap (hatched on diagram) from both pieces using a coping saw, band saw or jig saw, secure them together in your bench vice and finish off the curves with a file or sandpaper so that both pieces are identical. Keeping them together, turn them over in the vice and round off the bottom corners (diagram 5). Set aside.

Wheels

15. Using your compass set at a radius of 50 mm (2 in), mark out four circles for the wheels on the remaining piece of pine, leaving a comfortable space between them for a saw cut (see cutting plan). Make sure that you leave a good, visible centre point as you will need to drill through this for the axle. Cut out the four wheels carefully and accurately, sand the surfaces, and gently round the edges.

Handle

16. Mark two lengths of 600 mm (2 ft) on the 1250 mm (4 ft 1 in) length of pine, leaving at least 2 mm (¹⁄₁₆ in) between them for the saw cut. Using your compass set at half the width of the pine, draw a half circle at the end of each piece. Using a protractor, mark and draw an angle of 80° at the other end of each piece; mark in two pencil points for screw holes as indicated (diagram 8).

DIAGRAM 8

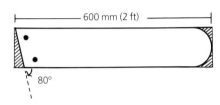

17. Cut these two pieces out and gently round all the edges with sandpaper so that you have two handle supports (diagram 9).

DIAGRAM 9

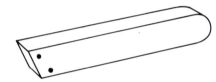

18. Now cut the dowel or broom handle so that it is the same length as the outside width measurement of the barrow. This measurement should be 320 mm (12½ in). Set aside for later.

Drilling holes

19. Drill the holes at the four points on each side piece, at one point on each end piece, at the centre point of each wheel, and at the three points on the handle supports. Carefully countersink all the holes on the outside surfaces so that the No. 10 screw heads for the wheels and the No 8. screw heads for the rest of the barrow will fit in neatly (diagram 10).

DIAGRAM 10

SCREW HEAD NEATLY COUNTERSUNK

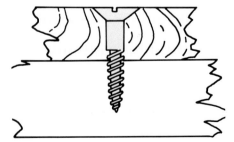

Wheel spacers

20. Draw four circles with a radius of 10 mm (⅜ in) on the plywood or hardwood, making sure that the centre point on each is clearly visible. Before cutting these four out, drill a hole at the centre point of each, large enough for the wheel screws to pass through. Cut the discs out, smooth the edges, and set aside for later.

Construction

21. Before assembling the barrow, clean all surfaces with sandpaper, leaving only a faint mark so that you can identify the face sides, edges, and so on.

22. Place the base piece on the flat surface of your bench and place one end piece in its correct position (diagram 11).

DIAGRAM 11

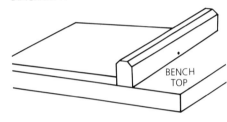

Using a bradawl, make a mark on the base piece through the hole in the end piece; this is the position for the retaining screw. Do the same on the other end. Secure the base piece in your bench vice with one end up, and drill a vertical lead hole at the mark. The drill bit used must be the same size as the shank of the screw you will use (diagram 12).

DIAGRAM 12

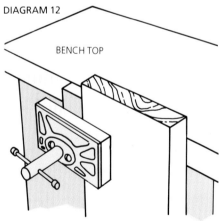

23. Smooth a thin layer of wood glue on the end of the base piece. Place the end piece in its correct position and screw home firmly. Any excess glue needs to be wiped away with a damp cloth immediately, otherwise, when you varnish the barrow, the varnish won't take on the glue patches and ugly blemishes will result.

24. Secure the other end piece by repeating the above steps. Place the base piece on your work-bench again, hold one of the side pieces in position and, using the bradawl, mark all the screw holes.

25. Secure the barrow in the bench vice, and fix the side pieces in the same way as the end pieces. Do not put a screw in point W (diagram 13) as this is the centre point for the wheel axle, the screw for which will go through the wheel, through the side piece, and into the end piece.

DIAGRAM 13

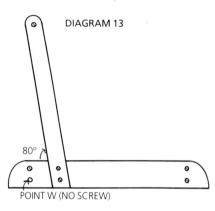

POINT W (NO SCREW)

26. Lay the barrow on one side and screw one of the handle supports into position, up against the 80° guideline (diagram 13).

27. Repeat for the other side and then, from one side of the barrow, look across the two supports to check that they are in line with each other. A few gentle taps with a mallet should correct any difference.

28. Take the length of dowel or broom handle, hold it in position at the top of the handle supports, and mark and drill the screw hole on each end. Put a touch of glue on each end of the handle and screw it into position, making sure that any surplus glue is wiped away.

29. All that remains to be done is to secure the wheels in position. First, rub the wheel spacers well with candle wax; this will ensure that they turn smoothly. Screw the wheels on tightly, and then gently undo the screws a half-turn or so until the wheels spin easily.

30. Remove the wheels and sand down the barrow and the blocks before applying three coats of varnish to all parts, *except the spacers*. Allow to dry. Sandpaper the barrow and blocks between each coat of varnish to create a smooth finish.

Spacers

31. Finally, replace the wheels and spacers, ensuring that the wheels move easily.

WHEELBARROW

This project is not quite as straightforward as it looks. It is, in fact, an exercise in cutting angles. But don't let this discourage you — providing you take your time and cut the angles accurately, you shouldn't have any problems. A radial-arm saw or other fixed saw, where an angle can be set, would be useful, but remember that there isn't very much that a machine can do that can't be done as well by a careful hand.

SKILL LEVEL 2

Body

Because most of the lines in this project are cut at an angle, cut the components for the body away from each other, but cut just clear of the lines. There are a number of angles that need to be cut and a description of how to measure angles and transfer these angles to the wood can be found on page 74, step 12, and diagrams 5b–5f .

Base

1. From the 1000 mm x 500 mm (3 ft 3 in x 1 ft 6 in) pine, cut out the base piece as shown (diagram 1a). Mark the face side on the top surface.

2. Drill one 4 mm (⅛ in) hole as marked (diagram 1a) and countersink it on the underside (the side without the face mark).

3. Cut the angles as marked (diagrams 1b & 1c) and set this piece aside.

Sides

4. Cut two pieces as shown (diagram 2a), drill four 4 mm (⅛ in) holes as marked, and countersink them on the outside surface to accommodate the head of a No. 10 screw.

5. Remembering that the sides are the same shape, but that the angles are on opposite sides, cut the necessary angles as marked (diagrams 2b & 2c).

Materials

1 x 1000 mm x 500 mm x 22 mm
  (3 ft 3 in x 1 ft 6 in x ⅞ in) piece pine
1 x 1700 mm x 30 mm x 30 mm
  (5 ft 6 in x 1¼ in x 1¼ in) piece pine
1 x 110 mm x 12 mm (4½ in x ½ in)
  dowel rod
2 x 20 mm (¾ in) No. 10 countersunk
  steel screws
1 x 30 mm (1¼ in) No. 10 countersunk
  steel screw

1 x 80 mm x 40 mm (3¼ in x 1¾ in) piece
  scrap hardboard
  (for the wheel spacers)
13 x 50 mm (2 in) No. 10 countersunk
  steel screws
Sandpaper
Wood glue
Wood filler
Wax candle
White universal undercoat
Topcoat paint

DIAGRAM 1a

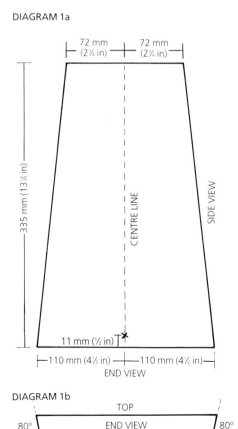

DIAGRAM 1c

DIAGRAM 2a

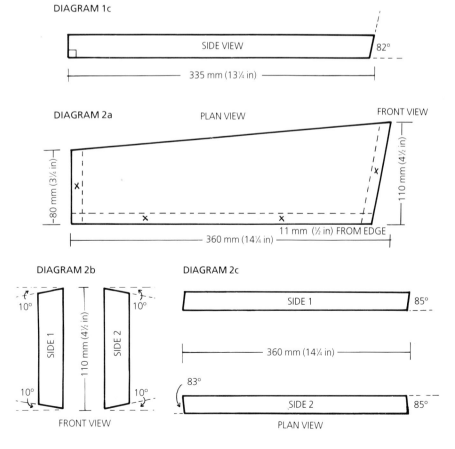

Front end piece

6. Cut the front end piece as shown (diagram 3), but draw in the curve first. This gentle curve can be drawn freehand. Marking it out as shown in the diagram will make this a lot easier.

DIAGRAM 3

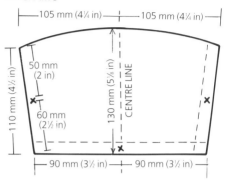

7. Drill three 4 mm (⅛ in) holes as marked, 12 mm (½ in) from the respective edges. Set aside for later. The angles on all edges of this piece are so gentle that it's probably better to leave them until you assemble the barrow and plane them off at that stage.

Back end piece

8. Cut this piece as shown (diagram 4a).

DIAGRAM 4a

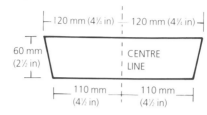

9. Cut the angles as shown (diagram 4b).

DIAGRAM 5

DIAGRAM 4b

PLAN VIEW

Frame

10. For the frame, cut two 700 mm (2 ft 3 in) long handles from the 1700 mm x 30 mm (5 ft 6 in x 1¼ in) length of pine. Decide which surface of each handle is going to be the outside surface and mark this with a face mark; this will always be the outside. Using a rasp and sandpaper, shape a hand hold at one end of each piece (diagram 5).

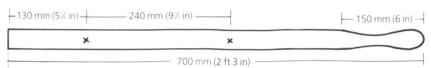

DIAGRAM 6

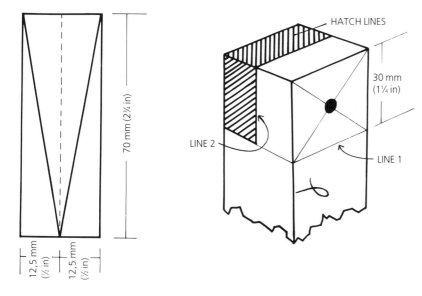

DIAGRAM 7

HATCH LINES

30 mm (1¼ in)

LINE 2

LINE 1

DIAGRAM 8

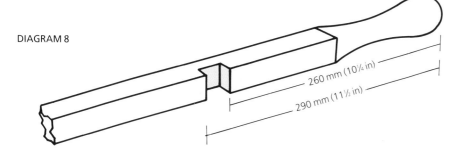

260 mm (10¼ in)

290 mm (11½ in)

(diagram 9). Hold these in position by placing a block on top of the assembly and clamping it to your work surface. On one side of the separators, drill two 4 mm (⅛ in) holes to a depth of 20 mm (¾ in).

21. Through the centre of each of these holes drill a slightly smaller hole to a depth of 40 mm (1¾ in), and then countersink these holes. Screw a 20 mm (¾ in) No. 8 screw into each hole.

22. Repeat on the other side.

DIAGRAM 9

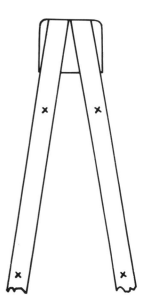

290 mm (11½ in)

23. Now take this assembly to pieces and construct using wood glue (diagram 9).

24. When the glue is thoroughly dry, use a rasp and sandpaper to round off the ends (diagram 10a).

DIAGRAM 10a

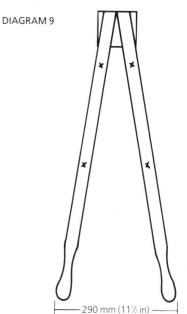

11. Measuring from the square end, drill two 4 mm (⅛ in) holes through each handle as marked (diagram 5) and countersink them on the underside.

12. Cut a rectangle 70 mm x 25 mm (2¾ in x 1 in) from the pine and mark lines on this piece (diagram 6). Using a tenon saw or a band saw cut along these lines so that the result is three separators, two of which will be identical. Carefully set these aside.

Legs
13. Cut two 120 mm (4¾ in) lengths from the remainder of the 30 mm x 30 mm (1¼ in x 1¼ in) pine. Decide which surface is going to be the outside and mark this surface with a face mark on each leg.

Jointing the legs to the handles
14. Measure 30 mm (1¼ in) from one end of each leg and square this line (line 1) right round (diagram 7).

15. Set your marking gauge at exactly half the thickness of the leg, mark a line (line 2) over the top of each leg, *measuring from the face side,* and pencil this in for clarity (diagram 7). On the side opposite the face

side, draw hatching lines to mark the scrap (diagram 7). Cut away the scrap, which has been hatched on diagram 7.

16. On the side that has not been cut away, draw in the diagonals and drill a 4 mm (⅛ in) hole through the centre spot, and countersink it on this side (diagram 7).

17. On each handle, measure 260 mm (10¼ in) and then 290 mm (11½ in) from the end of the hand hold and square these two lines right round.

18. Using your marking gauge (which is still set at half the leg thickness), mark the top and bottom surfaces of each handle, ensuring that you mark from the face side (diagram 8). Hatch in the scrap side (the side opposite the face side) and cut it away.

19. The legs should now fit snugly into the handles and be flush with all the surfaces. If not, make adjustments, checking the fit frequently, until you're satisfied.

Fitting the frame together
20. Lay the handles and the three separators made in step 12 on your work surface

25. Drill the axle hole right through the frame at the position marked (diagram 10b). You will need to use a drill bit that is about 2 mm (1/16 in) wider than the width of the dowel rod you are using.

DIAGRAM 10b

Fitting the legs to the frame

26. Check that the legs fit snugly in the frame; now apply a thin coat of glue to the surfaces that will meet, and slip the leg into place.

27. Drill a 2 mm (1/16 in) lead hole through the main hole and screw a 20 mm (3/4 in) No. 10 screw into place. Check, using your square, that each leg is square to the frame (diagram 11).

DIAGRAM 11

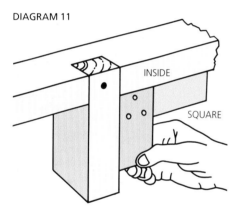

Wheels

28. Using a compass, draw two circles with a radius of 50 mm (2 in) on a remaining piece of pine, making sure that the centre spot of each circle is clearly visible. Using a coping saw, a band saw or a jig saw, cut out the two circles. Using a rasp and sandpaper, make the wheels as circular as possible and round off the edges.

29. At the exact centre point of each wheel, drill a 12 mm (1/2 in) hole *but only to half the thickness of the wheel.* This will be the retaining hole for the axle. Set these aside.

Spacers

30. Draw two circles, each with a radius of 15 mm (5/8 in) on the small piece of hardboard, making sure that the centre point of each circle is clearly visible. Drill a hole through the centre point using a drill

bit that is 2 mm (1/16 in) wider than the width of the dowel. Cut out these two circles, smooth them all round with sandpaper and set aside for later.

Construction

We shall first fit the wheelbarrow together without any glue, to ensure that everything fits together well. If any adjustments are necessary, they can be made at this stage.

Remember that each screw will require a lead hole. Use a drill bit that is the same width as the shaft of the screw; in the case of No. 10 screws, a 3 mm (1/8 in) bit should be satisfactory. The lead hole will need to be the same length as the depth to which the screw is going to penetrate into the wood.

31. Fit the back end piece to the base.

32. Now fit both side pieces to the base, before fitting the front end piece into position. At this stage, adjust angles and edges with a plane or rasp if necessary, so that all edges and corners on the body of the barrow are nicely rounded.

33. Place the body upside-down on your work surface and place the frame on it, ensuring that the legs are facing away from the body. If the front of the frame protrudes 11 mm (1/2 in) from the front of the body, you should be able to see that screws fitted through the holes in the frame will go directly into the front end piece, through the base, and into the back end piece (diagram 12).

DIAGRAM 12

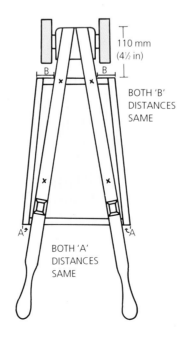

34. Check that the frame is positioned exactly in the centre of the width of the body, then drill the lead holes and secure the frame to the base.

35. Insert the axle through its hole, slip a spacer over each end, followed by a wheel.

You should now have a functioning wheelbarrow that looks like the one in the photograph, except for the paint.

36. Take the barrow to pieces and then repeat the construction steps described above, applying a thin layer of wood glue to each surface to be joined. Make sure that you wipe away any excess glue with a wet cloth. *Do not* fit the axle and wheels until the rest of the barrow and the wheels have been painted.

37. Fill all the countersunk holes with wood filler and, when this is thoroughly dry, sand the excess filler so that the filled holes are flush with the surrounding wood.

38. When you're satisfied that everything is as it should be, give the entire structure a thorough sanding, making sure that every surface, edge and corner is smooth and pleasant to the touch.

Painting and finishing

39. Give the whole structure and the wheels, *but not the axle,* a coat of white undercoat.

40. When this is thoroughly dry, give all surfaces a good rub over with a fine sandpaper.

41. Apply the topcoat in the colour of your choice. You might find that it is necessary to apply two topcoats for a really good finish. Each coat must be thoroughly dry and then rubbed down with fine sandpaper before applying the next.

42. When the final coat of paint is dry, rub the axle to within 20 mm (3/4 in) of each end with an ordinary household candle. This will act as a lubricant.

43. Put a *small* quantity of glue on one end of the axle and insert it firmly into one of the wheels, making sure that it is square on the axle.

44. When this is dry, insert a spacer over the axle, and feed the axle through the axle hole. Add the second spacer and put a *small* quantity of glue on the extreme end of the axle. Firmly push the wheel on, making sure that it is square on the axle and that the wheel/axle assembly spins smoothly.

An endless variety of games that will keep children occupied for hours can be invented using these push-and-pull toys.

HELICOPTER

Things that move fascinate children — especially if they are realistic. This helicopter, with its rotor and tail rotor that spin around, will give hours of pleasure.

SKILL LEVEL 1–2

Materials

1 x 370 mm x 75 mm x 35 mm
 (14½ in x 3 in x 1½ in) piece pine
1 x 250 mm x 12 mm x 5 mm
 (10 in x ½ in x ¼ in) piece pine
2 x 225 mm x 10 mm (9 in x ⅜ in)
 dowel rods
2 x 30 mm (1¼ in) No. 10 countersunk
 steel screws
4 x 15 mm (⅝ in) No. 6 countersunk
 steel screws
1 x 15 mm (⅝ in) No. 6 round-headed
 steel screw
1 x 10 mm (⅜ in) No. 6 round-headed
 steel screw
2 x 10 mm (⅜ in) electrical washers
Sandpaper
Wood glue
Wood filler
White universal undercoat
Topcoat paint

Body

1. Enlarge diagram 1 to full size (280 mm [11 in] long), either freehand or on a photocopier and transfer on to the larger piece of pine by placing carbon paper under the enlarged diagram and following the outline with a pencil. Don't forget to draw in the cockpit at the same time.

2. Using a band saw, coping saw or jig saw, cut out the body; diagram 2 shows a top view of this piece. Follow this diagram and draw the shape of the cockpit and the tapering tail on to the wood.

DIAGRAM 1

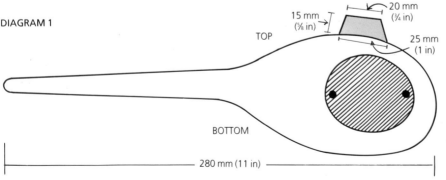

DIAGRAM 2   PLAN VIEW

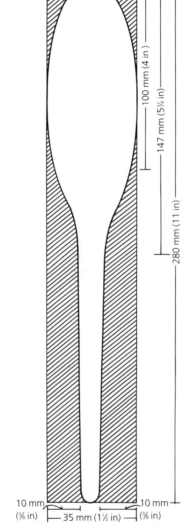

3. Using the same saw, cut away the scrap, indicated by hatching lines on diagram 2.

4. Drill two lead holes (represented by the black dots on diagram 1), then use a jig saw or a keyhole saw to cut out the hole for the cockpit. The lead holes will need to be a few millimetres larger than the width of the blade you will use.

5. Using a rasp and sandpaper, round all the edges and surfaces to make the body as realistic as possible (see photograph).

Undercarriage

6. Cut a piece from the remainder of the pine following diagram 3. This can be traced on to the wood in the same way as the body. Ensure that the measurements are full size.

DIAGRAM 3

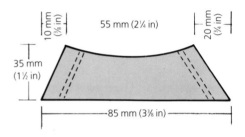

7. Draw the angles on both front and back (diagram 4), continue the lines along the top surface of the wood, and then plane away the scrap.

DIAGRAM 4

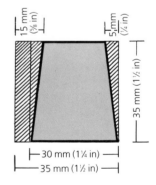

8. Hold this piece up against the bottom surface of the helicopter body and, using a rasp, shape the top surface of the undercarriage until the two pieces fit snugly together. If you place the undercarriage on a flat surface, the tail of the helicopter should be angled away from the horizontal (diagram 5).

DIAGRAM 5

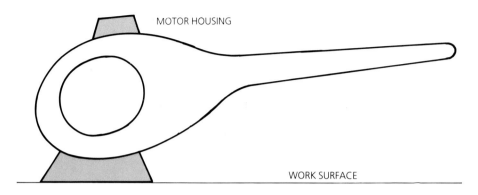

MOTOR HOUSING

WORK SURFACE

Main rotor blade

13. Cut a 180 mm (7 in) length from the thin — 5 mm (¼ in) — piece of pine. Drill a 3 mm (⅛ in) hole right through the centre of the width and length of the rotor. This will be the axis on which the rotor spins, so it's important that this hole is dead centre. Using sandpaper, round off the ends and all the edges of this piece to make it look as realistic as possible. However, remember that this toy will be used by a child and if the rotor is too thin, it will break.

Tail rotor

14. Cut a 60 mm (2½ in) length from the remainder of the 5 mm (¼ in) thick pine, and follow the same steps as for the main rotor blade, above.

Construction

We shall first assemble the helicopter 'dry', that is, without any glue, ensuring that everything fits together well. Remember, too, that before a screw can be screwed into place, a lead hole has to be drilled. For this you will need a drill bit that is the same width as the shank of the screw. The retaining hole must be the same depth as the distance the screw will protrude from the main hole.

15. Screw the undercarriage to the body (diagram 5).

16. Screw the skids to the undercarriage so that from the front it looks like diagram 8a and from the side it looks like diagram 8b.

DIAGRAM 6a

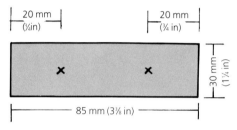

20 mm (¾ in)   20 mm (¾ in)

30 mm (1¼ in)

85 mm (3⅜ in)

DIAGRAM 6b

9. Drill a 4 mm (⅛ in) hole at each end of the bottom of the undercarriage so that the angle of the hole follows the angle of the end of the undercarriage (diagram 3). Diagram 6a shows a view of the underside and diagram 6b is a cross section through the undercarriage. Countersink these holes on the underside to accommodate the head of a No. 10 screw.

Skids

10. For the skids, cut two 125 mm (5 in) lengths from one of the dowels and round off the ends with sandpaper.

11. Clamp each skid to your work surface and drill two 3 mm (⅛ in) vertical holes in each, one 30 mm (1¼ in) from one end and the other 50 mm (2 in) from the other end. Carefully countersink these holes on one side only to accommodate the head of a No. 6 screw.

Motor housing

12. Cut the motor housing (diagram 7a) from a remaining piece of pine. The front view is given in diagram 7b. Using a rasp, file the longest surface of the motor housing concave, so that it fits on top of the body as in diagram 5, above.

DIAGRAM 8a

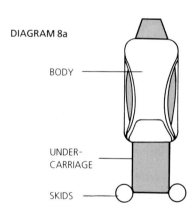

BODY

UNDER-
CARRIAGE

SKIDS

DIAGRAM 7a

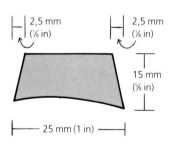

2,5 mm (⅛ in)   2,5 mm (⅛ in)

15 mm (⅝ in)

25 mm (1 in)

DIAGRAM 7b

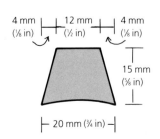

4 mm (⅛ in)   12 mm (½ in)   4 mm (⅛ in)

15 mm (⅝ in)

20 mm (¾ in)

DIAGRAM 8b

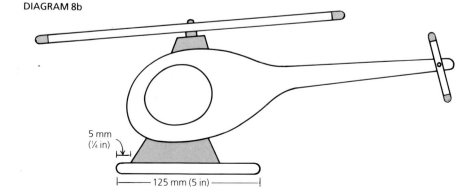

5 mm (¼ in)

125 mm (5 in)

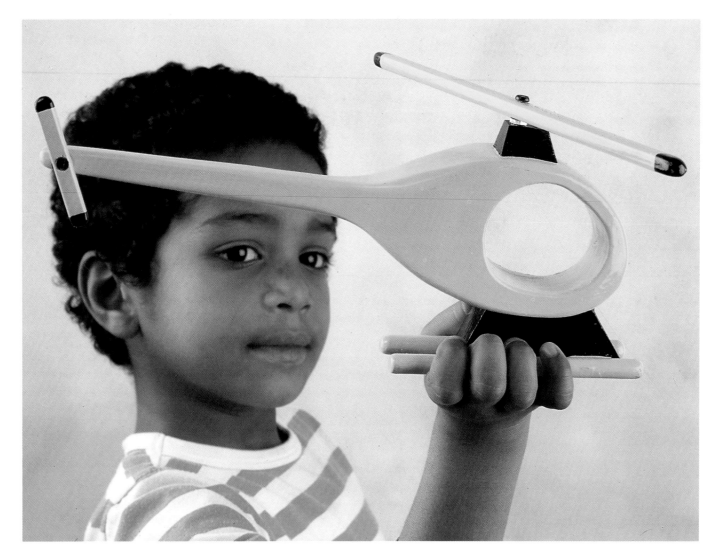

The slight height of the undercarriage above the ground can be achieved by placing a thin piece of plywood on the work surface. The undercarriage will stand on this wood, while the skid will be on the work surface itself (diagram 9). Do not attach the plywood to the undercarriage — it is used simply to create height while fixing the skids. This will also mean that the screw holes will be angled slightly upwards, towards the undercarriage.

17. Screw the motor housing to the centre of the body so that its top surface leans slightly forward (diagram 8b).

18. Drill a 2 mm (¹⁄₁₆ in) lead hole into the dead centre of the top of the motor housing. With a washer between the housing and the rotor, screw the rotor into place so that it spins freely.

19. Carefully drill a 2 mm (¹⁄₁₆ in) lead hole 5 mm (¼ in) from the end of the tail of the body, noting from the photograph which side to attach it to, and with a washer between it and the body, screw the tail rotor into position so that it spins freely.

DIAGRAM 9

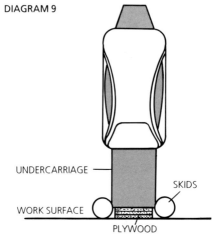

UNDERCARRIAGE

SKIDS

WORK SURFACE

PLYWOOD

20. When you're certain that everything fits perfectly, take the toy to pieces, give every part a final sanding to ensure a good finish and assemble the chopper using a thin layer of wood glue on each surface to be joined. Make sure that any surplus glue is wiped off with a damp cloth. Do not, at this stage, attach either of the rotors as this will make painting very difficult.

Painting and final construction
21. Give every surface a coat of universal white undercoat. (It may be a good idea to put a knotted string through the centre hole of each rotor so that they can be suspended while the paint dries. In the same way, you could screw a cup hook into the hole in the top of the motor housing so that it, too, can be suspended while the paint dries.) When the undercoat is thoroughly dry, rub down all parts gently with sandpaper to remove irregularities.

22. Apply the topcoat of your choice. You may find it necessary to apply two topcoats to achieve a really good finish. It might be a good idea to add some decoration at the end of the rotors (see photograph), but remember that each coat must be thoroughly dry before attempting to apply another over, or alongside it.

23. Finally, screw the main rotor back into position, making sure that it's tight enough not to wobble, while at the same time being free to spin smoothly. In the same way, screw the tail rotor into position.

BLOCK POLE

This simple and easily made toy is a standard favourite that helps to develop hand-eye coordination, as well as a concept of size and number, and it's also fun to play with. Not much wood is needed and most of the pieces are small, so you may well be able to use up some scrap wood, instead of throwing it on the fire.

SKILL LEVEL 1

Materials

1 x 300 mm x 220 mm x 22 mm (12 in x 8¾ in x ⅞ in) piece pine
1 x 155 mm x 10 mm (6⅛ in x ⅜ in) dowel rod
Sandpaper
Wood glue
Varnish OR wood finish

1. Before cutting out the components, draw them all on the board, ensuring that all corners are square, and that you will have enough wood.

Blocks and base

2. Draw and then cut out one block of each of the following sizes:
- 120 mm x 120 mm (4¾ in x 4¾ in) (to be used for the base)
- 100 mm x 100 mm (4 in x 4 in)
- 90 mm x 90 mm (3½ in x 3½ in)
- 80 mm x 80 mm (3¼ in x 3¼ in)
- 70 mm x 70 mm (2¾ in x 2¾ in)
- 60 mm x 60 mm (2½ in x 2½ in)
- 50 mm x 50 mm (2 in x 2 in)

3. On each piece, draw in the diagonals on one surface (diagram 1). This will give you the centre point into which to drill the hole.

DIAGRAM 1

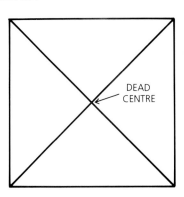

DEAD CENTRE

4. On the base piece, drill a 10 mm (⅜ in) hole, 15 mm (⅝ in) deep, where the diagonals cross.

5. Drill a 12 mm (½ in) hole in the dead centre of the remaining blocks.

6. Using a rasp and sandpaper, or a router, round off only the top edges of the base piece (with the hole uppermost). Round off all the edges and corners of all the other blocks. Using fine sandpaper, sand all the components smooth and clean, ensuring that you remove all pencil marks.

Pin

7. For the pin, round off one end of the dowel rod with a rasp and sandpaper.

Construction

8. Smear a small quantity of wood glue on the square end of the dowel rod and, using a mallet, tap the dowel rod into the hole in the base piece. Using a square, check that the dowel rod is square to the base, from all directions. Wipe away any excess glue with a damp cloth. If this is not removed promptly it will prevent the varnish from penetrating the wood at the points where the glue has dried, and the finished appearance of the toy will be spoiled.

Finishing

9. This toy looks great finished with varnish or a good wood finish, so apply three coats to every component except the dowel rod. Remember that when each coat is dry it must be sanded down with fine sandpaper before the next coat is applied. When all the components are thoroughly dry, the toy can be assembled.

NUMBER STACK

This is a good educational toy that helps youngsters to visualize numerical values up to five. Don't be deceived by its apparent simplicity — it's not as easy to make as it looks! The secret is accurate measuring and drilling. A drill press will make the job much easier but a hand-held electric drill, or even a manual drill, is quite adequate, if you take your time and work carefully.

Two choices of wood exist here — pine or MDF board. Pine looks better, but on a small-scale project like this one is more difficult to work accurately than MDF board.

Whichever wood you choose, you will need the same size board.

SKILL LEVEL 2

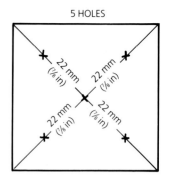

DIAGRAM 2

5 HOLES

22 mm (⅞ in) 22 mm (⅞ in) 22 mm (⅞ in) 22 mm (⅞ in)

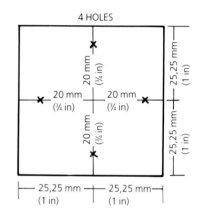

DIAGRAM 3

4 HOLES

20 mm (¾ in) · 20 mm (¾ in) · 20 mm (¾ in) · 20 mm (¾ in)

25,25 mm (1 in) · 25,25 mm (1 in)

25,25 mm (1 in) · 25,25 mm (1 in)

Materials
1 x 500 mm x 200 mm x 22 mm
   (1 ft 6 in x 8 in x ⅞ in) piece pine OR
1 x 500 mm x 200 mm x 12 mm
   (1 ft 6 in x 8 in x ½ in) MDF board
1 x 1500 mm x 10 mm (5 ft x ⅜ in)
   dowel rod
Sandpaper
Wood glue
Varnish OR
White universal undercoat and
Topcoat paint

Cutting the base
1. Cut a simple 401 mm x 71 mm (1 ft 3 in x 2¾ in) rectangle and draw pencil lines on the top surface as in diagram 1.

Cutting the blocks
The blocks need to be cut accurately. A radial-arm saw or circular saw with a guide fitted to the bed will ensure that the blocks are the same size and square. However, if you draw and cut the squares accurately, this can be achieved with a hand saw.

2. Cut two strips 55 mm (2¼ in) wide. Set your saw to cut 15 blocks, measuring 55 mm x 55 mm (2¼ in x 2¼ in).

Drilling the blocks
3. For the blocks to fit easily over the pins, it is essential that the holes are drilled exactly on the marks. Mark and drill the required number of 14 mm (½ in) holes through each of the 15 blocks (diagrams 2–6).

You will need:
• 5 of diagram 2
• 4 of diagram 3
• 3 of diagram 4
• 2 of diagram 5
• 1 of diagram 6

DIAGRAM 4

3 HOLES

20 mm (¾ in) · 20 mm (¾ in)

DIAGRAM 5

2 HOLES

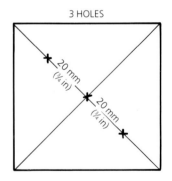

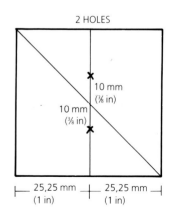

10 mm (⅜ in)

10 mm (⅜ in)

25,25 mm (1 in) · 25,25 mm (1 in)

DIAGRAM 1

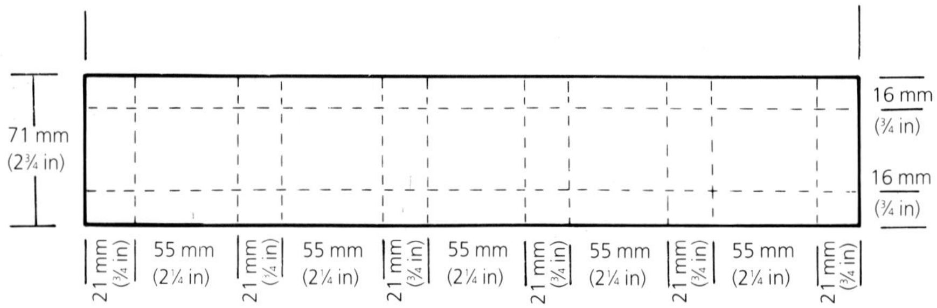

71 mm (2¾ in)

16 mm (¾ in)

16 mm (¾ in)

21 mm (¾ in) · 55 mm (2¼ in) · 21 mm (¾ in) · 55 mm (2¼ in) · 21 mm (¾ in) · 55 mm (2¼ in) · 21 mm (¾ in) · 55 mm (2¼ in) · 21 mm (¾ in) · 55 mm (2¼ in) · 21 mm (¾ in)

DIAGRAM 6

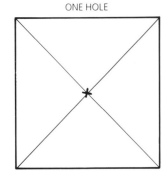

ONE HOLE

Drilling the base
4. As you did for the blocks, mark out each square on the base, one for each size, in descending order from five holes to one hole (diagram 7).

DIAGRAM 7

| 1 | 2 | 3 | 4 | 5 |

5. Place one of each kind of block on the base, over the appropriate number of holes to check that the holes have been drilled in the correct places. Drill a 10 mm (⅜ in) hole, 5 mm (¼ in) deep, exactly on each mark. The holes must be drilled accurately.

Pins
6. Before cutting the dowel, accurately mark the lengths of all the pins on the

dowel to the sizes listed below, ensuring that you plan correctly before cutting — there's nothing more frustrating than having sufficient wood to start with, but cutting it out uneconomically and then not having enough for completion. If you are using pine, the first size applies. If you're using MDF board, the second size applies.

- Cut 5 x 115 mm; 70 mm (4½ in; 2¾ in) lengths of dowel.
- Cut 4 x 95 mm; 58 mm (3¾ in; 2¼ in) lengths of dowel.
- Cut 3 x 75 mm; 46 mm (3 in; 1¾ in) lengths of dowel.
- Cut 2 x 55 mm; 34 mm (2¼ in; 1¼ in) lengths of dowel.
- Cut 1 x 35 mm; 22 mm (1¼ in; ⅞ in) length of dowel.

7. Using a rasp and sandpaper, round off one end of each dowel pin.

Construction
8. First assemble the toy without any glue, ensuring that everything fits together well. Using a mallet, gently tap the five longest pins into the five holes, the four next in size into the four holes and so on, until all the pins are in place. Drop the

appropriate blocks over the pins. If everything has been cut accurately the job will now look good, except for the fact that it needs a clean-up.

9. When you're satisfied that all is well, take the job to pieces and, using a rasp and sandpaper, a router or a spindle cutter, round off all the corners of the base and blocks. Sand these pieces smooth and clean (so that there are no pencil marks left).

10. Now apply a small amount of wood glue to the square end of each pin and, one at a time, tap them into place. As each pin is tapped into place, use a square to check that it is square to the base in all respects.

Finishing
11. If you have used pine, your number stack will look better varnished than painted. Apply three coats of good varnish, remembering to sand down each coat with fine sandpaper when thoroughly dry, before applying the next coat.

12. If you've used MDF board, a painted finish will probably look better, so apply a coat of undercoat to all the components except the pins, as paint will be a bit too thick for them. When the undercoat is dry, apply the topcoat in a colour of your choice. It might be a good idea to paint each stack a different colour, which will help with identification. You may have to apply two topcoats to achieve a really good finish, but the extra time and effort will be worth it. Remember to ensure that each coat is thoroughly dry before sanding down with fine sandpaper and applying another coat.

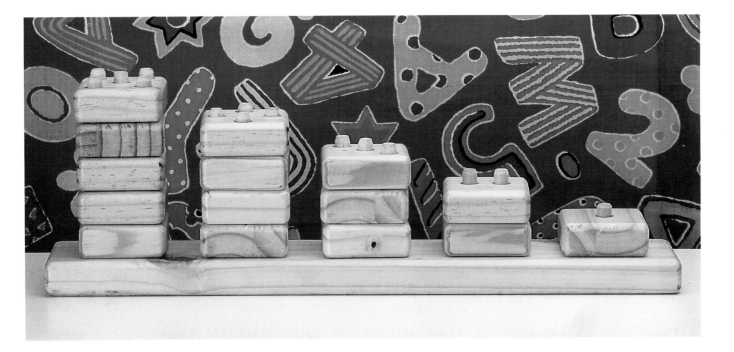

THREADNEEDLE

This unusual toy will provide lots of enjoyment for children. It involves threading the needle through the block in an infinite variety of ways, forming interesting patterns, and then reversing the process and starting again.

SKILL LEVEL 1

Materials
1 x 170 mm x 60 mm x 50 mm
   (6¾ in x 2½ in x 2 in) piece pine
   (a hardwood such as oak or beech will
   look very good and will probably last
   a lot longer)
1 x 100 mm x 10 mm (4 in x ⅜ in)
   dowel rod
500 mm (½ yd) x 4 mm (⅛ in)
   terylene line
Sandpaper
Wood glue
Varnish OR wood finish

Block
1. Clamp the block of pine to your work surface, narrow side up, with scrap wood between the work surface and the block. Using a 14 mm (½ in) drill bit, drill three holes vertically through the block in the positions indicated (diagram 1).

2. Turn the block broad side up and drill four holes vertically through the block in the positions indicated (diagram 2).

3. Keeping the block in this position, drill two or three holes at random, yet evenly spaced angles through the block, trying not to penetrate any of the other holes. Turn the block narrow side up again and repeat this process.

4. With the block in the same position, drill a 3 mm (⅛ in) hole, 50 mm (2 in) deep, vertical to the surface in one corner (point 1 on diagram 2). This will be the retaining hole for the line.

5. Plane and sand the block smooth, rounding off all the corners and edges.

Needle
6. For the needle, drill a 4 mm (⅛ in) vertical hole, 50 mm (2 in) deep, in the centre of one end of the dowel rod and, with a rasp and sandpaper, round off this end until only a narrow rim is left around the hole. (This will help when the needle is pulled back through the holes in the block.)

7. At the other end of this rod, taper the end to resemble the end of a needle, using a rasp and sandpaper.
Warning! Don't make the end too sharp as it could be dangerous.

Finishing
8. Sand down the block and the needle with fine sandpaper before applying three coats of varnish or wood finish. Each coat must be thoroughly dry before it is sanded down and the next coat is applied.

Construction
9. Apply a strong glue to 50 mm (2 in) of each end of the terylene line. Insert one end 4 mm (⅛ in) into the retaining hole at the corner of the block, and insert the other end into the hole in the needle. Allow the glue to dry completely.

DIAGRAM 1

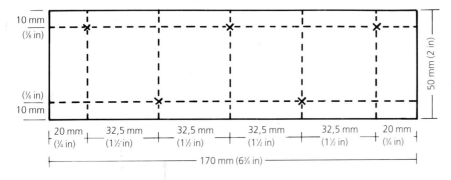

| | 10 mm (⅜ in) | | | | | 50 mm (2 in) |

20 mm (¾ in)   32,5 mm (1½ in)   32,5 mm (1½ in)   32,5 mm (1½ in)   32,5 mm (1½ in)   20 mm (¾ in)

170 mm (6¾ in)

DIAGRAM 2

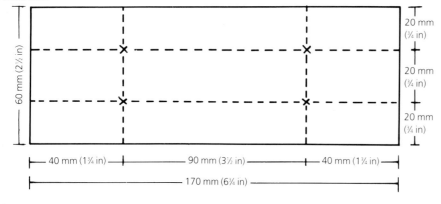

60 mm (2½ in)

20 mm (¾ in)
20 mm (¾ in)
20 mm (¾ in)

40 mm (1¾ in)   90 mm (3½ in)   40 mm (1¾ in)

170 mm (6¾ in)

These toys have been designed to develop hand-eye co-ordination and number concepts, making them useful educational aids.

PEG BOARD

This toy is popular with young children because they can hammer the living daylights out of it! It also helps to develop hand-eye coordination, making it a useful educational toy.

SKILL LEVEL 1

Materials

1 x 250 mm x 200 mm x 12 mm (10 in x 8 in x ½ in) MDF board
1 x 350 mm x 10 mm (13¾ in x ⅜ in) dowel rod
1 x 50 mm x 25 mm (2 in x 1 in) dowel rod
1 x 110 mm x 12 mm (4½ in x ½ in) dowel rod
6 x 20 mm (¾ in) panel pins
Sandpaper
Wood glue
White universal undercoat
Topcoat paint
Varnish

1. Draw the board and supports on the MDF board before cutting out to ensure that you have used the wood efficiently, or you could discover that you don't have enough.

Board

2. For the board, cut one 200 mm x 80 mm (8 in x 3¼ in) rectangle and mark the pencil crosses on it as in diagram 1.

3. Before drilling the holes described below, take a piece of scrap and drill a hole, 10 mm (⅜ in) in diameter, through it. Now try fitting the 10 mm (⅜ in) dowel into this hole — it should be a tight fit, but a few light taps with a mallet should enable you to lightly hammer the dowel backwards and forwards. When this is working, drill a hole, 10 mm (⅜ in) in diameter, through the board at each of the marked crosses. Using a rasp and sandpaper, smooth off all the corners and edges.

Supports

4. For the supports, cut two 140 mm x 80 mm (5½ in x 3¼ in) rectangles from the MDF board. Following diagram 2, draw two parallel pencil lines —12 mm (½ in) apart — across one surface of each piece and square these down each side of the wood.

5. On each side of the wood, mark a depth line of 3 mm (⅛ in) and check that the lines you have drawn across the surface are exactly the same thickness as the board. Using a tenon saw, and starting your cut on the inside of the lines, cut vertically along the lines down to a depth of 3 mm (⅛ in).

6. Using a 10 mm (⅜ in) wide chisel, chisel out the scrap wood, ensuring that the bottom of the resulting groove is uniformly 3 mm (⅛ in) deep throughout. The ends of the peg board should fit exactly into this groove (diagram 3). Using a rasp and sandpaper, smooth the corners and edges.

Pegs

7. Cut five 75 mm (3 in) lengths from the 10 mm (⅜ in) dowel rod and round off the ends with sandpaper. Check that they fit snugly into the holes in the board. If they're too loose (which probably means that your drill wobbled) use 12 mm (½ in) pegs and sand them down until they fit snugly.

Hammer head

8. Mark 25 mm (1 in) in from one end of the 25 mm (1 in) dowel rod. Drill a 12 mm (½ in) hole, 15 mm (⅝ in) deep, vertical to the length of the head. Using a rasp and sandpaper, round off the ends of the head.

DIAGRAM 1

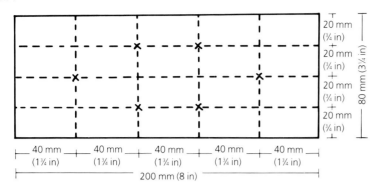

20 mm
(¾ in)

20 mm
(¾ in)

20 mm
(¾ in)

20 mm
(¾ in)

20 mm
(¾ in)

80 mm (3¼ in)

40 mm
(1¾ in)

40 mm
(1¾ in)

40 mm
(1¾ in)

40 mm
(1¾ in)

40 mm
(1¾ in)

200 mm (8 in)

DIAGRAM 2

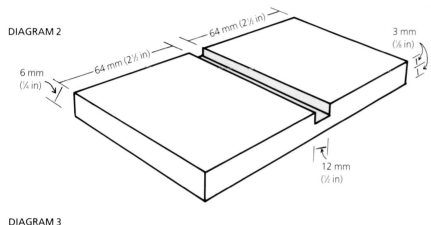

64 mm (2½ in)

64 mm (2½ in)

3 mm
(⅛ in)

6 mm
(¼ in)

12 mm
(½ in)

DIAGRAM 3

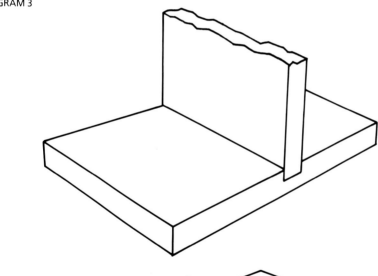

DIAGRAM 4

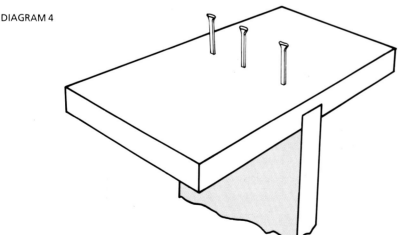

Hammer handle

9. Round off one end of the 110 mm x 12 mm (4½ in x ½ in) dowel rod with sandpaper. This handle should fit snugly into the hole in the head to form a complete little hammer.

Construction of board

10. Check that the ends of the board fit snugly into the supports, then fix it upright in your bench vice. Apply a thin coat of wood glue to completely cover the inner surface of one of the grooves and, using a mallet, tap the end into place on the board, ensuring that the sides of the support and the sides of the board are flush (diagram 4).

11. Hammer three panel pins into place (diagram 4). Make sure that you hammer the pins in vertically and until the head of each one is flush with the surface of the surrounding wood.

12. Remove the job from your bench vice and wipe away any surplus glue with a damp cloth. Using a square, check that the support is exactly square to the board. If it isn't, it can be gently adjusted by hand. Repeat the above for the other end.

Construction of hammer

13. When you're happy that the handle of the hammer fits snugly into the head, apply a little wood glue to the square end of the handle and tap this into position with a mallet. Using a square, check that the handle is square to the head in all respects. Adjustments can be made by hand at this stage. Wipe away any excess glue with a damp cloth, and leave to dry.

Painting

14. Sand down all components with fine sandpaper.

15. Give the peg board a coat of undercoat; when this is thoroughly dry, sand down with fine sandpaper.

16. Apply a topcoat in the colour of your choice. You will probably need to apply two topcoats to get a really good finish. Remember that when each coat is thoroughly dry, you need to sand it down before applying the next. Make sure that the holes in the peg board are clear of any paint drips that may have crept in during the painting process.

17. Give the hammer three coats of varnish, remembering to sand between coats.

18. When the paint is thoroughly dry, fit the pegs into the holes.

BLACKBOARD & EASEL

Most kids love drawing and painting. Here's a very practical toy that serves both as a blackboard and a painting easel, with the added benefit that there won't be any arguments as to whose turn it is, because there's room for two.

SKILL LEVEL 2

Materials

1 x 1700 mm x 380 mm x 22 mm
  (5 ft 6 in x 15 in x ⅞ in) piece pine
1 x 1225 mm x 1250 mm x 12 mm
  (4 ft x 4 ft 1 in x ½ in) MDF board
24 x 30 mm (1¼ in) No. 8 countersunk
  steel screws
12 x 30 mm (1¼ in) No. 6 countersunk
  steel screws
2 m (2 yds) 7 mm (¼ in) nylon rope
2 x 35 mm (1½ in) steel butt hinges
Sandpaper
4 plastic yoghurt cups OR
  similar containers
Wood filler
White universal undercoat
Topcoat paint
Matt black paint

Legs

1. Cut four 1000 mm x 60 mm (3 ft 3 in x 2½ in) legs from the pine using a radial-arm or cross-cut saw. Mark the face side on each piece (diagram 1).

DIAGRAM 1

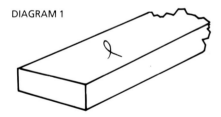

2. There will be two pairs of legs, so the following diagrams show the legs in pairs, and they must be marked and drilled as pairs. Draw pencil lines on the legs and drill four 4 mm (⅛ in) holes at the positions marked with a cross on diagram 2a, and countersink the holes on the face side to accommodate the head of a No. 8 screw.

3. Draw pencil lines on the legs as shown, drill two 3 mm (⅛ in) holes at the positions marked with a cross on diagram 2b, and countersink the holes on the face side to accommodate the head of a No. 6 screw.

DIAGRAM 2a

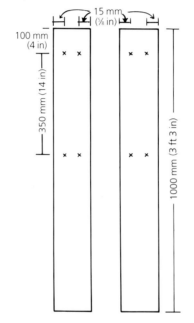

DIAGRAM 2b

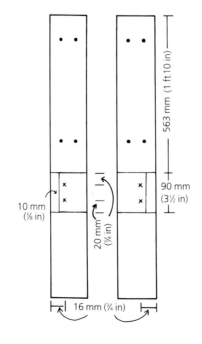

4. Draw pencil lines as shown and drill one 10 mm (⅜ in) hole at the position marked by the centre crosses on diagram 2c.

DIAGRAM 2c

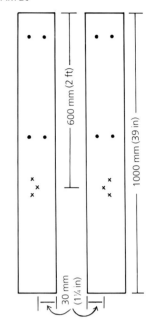

5. Using a hand plane, plane all the narrow edges smooth and lightly chamfer the corners so that from an end view they look like diagram 3.

DIAGRAM 3

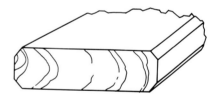

Boards

6. Cut two 600 mm x 550 mm (2 ft x 1 ft 8 in) rectangles from the MDF board. Using a hand plane, smooth the edges and chamfer them on one side only, so that the edges look like the edges on diagram 4.

DIAGRAM 4

Pot holders

7. Cut two 600 mm x 100 mm (2 ft x 4 in) rectangles from the MDF board.

8. Using a compass set to a radius of 20 mm (¾ in), draw two rounded corners on each piece (diagram 5).

9. The diameter of the pot-retaining holes, which you are about to draw, will depend on the size of the paint pots you have. We've used empty 175 ml (6 oz) plastic yoghurt cups, which are tapered and therefore fit snugly. Draw lines on the two boards as indicated by the dotted lines (diagram 5). Set a compass to the required diameter, and draw four circles from the points where the lines cross (diagram 5).

10. Drill a lead hole on the inside of each of the four circles; these have been indicated on the diagram by large dots. This will be the starter hole from which to cut out the retaining hole. The starter hole will need to be a couple of millimetres wider than the blade of the saw you will use.

11. Using a jig saw or keyhole saw, cut out these circles as accurately as possible.

12. Using a rasp, or a router and sandpaper, gently round off the edges of these holes and the edges of the piece itself, with the exception of the long straight edge, which will be the back.

Supports

13. Cut two pieces from the pine as shown in diagram 6 and, using a rasp and sandpaper, round off the edges along the side marked 'side 1'.

Clamps

14. Cut two 480 mm x 45 mm (1 ft 5 in x 1¾ in) rectangles from the MDF board.

15. Drill two 4 mm (⅛ in) holes in each piece as shown (diagram 7).

Construction

16. Assemble the job without glue, ensuring that everything fits together well and looks good. If any adjustments need to be made, this is the time to make them.

Fitting the legs

17. To fit the legs to the boards, lay one of the MDF boards on your work surface, with the chamfered side downwards. Lay one of the legs in position, with the counter-sinkings facing upwards and the two small holes closest to you (diagram 8). Fit flush with the top edge (the 600 mm [2 ft] edge) and flush with the side (diagram 9).

DIAGRAM 5

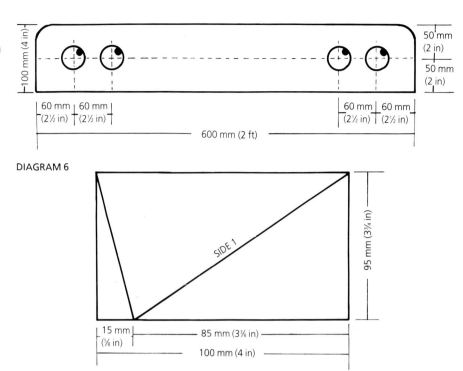

DIAGRAM 6

DIAGRAM 7

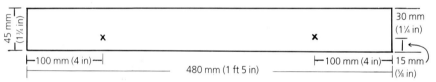

DIAGRAM 8

DIAGRAM 10

DIAGRAM 9

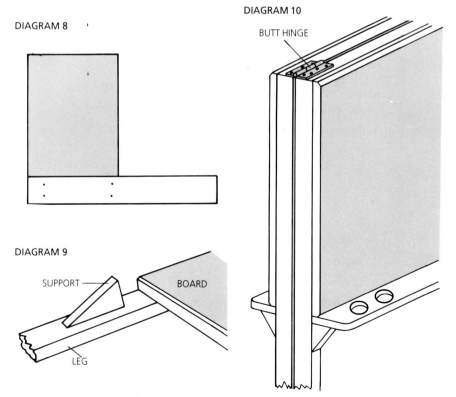

18. Clamp these two pieces together on to your work surface and check again that the edges are exactly flush. Drill lead holes for the four screws to fix the leg to the board. The lead hole must be the same width as the shank of the screw and must not be any deeper than half the thickness of the board.

19. Screw the four 30 mm (1¼ in) No. 8 screws into position.

20. Spin the top around on the work surface and repeat this exercise for the other leg. Set this piece aside.

21. Repeat the above instructions to attach the legs to the other board.

Fitting the supports
22. Fix one of the sections you've just completed in your bench vice, with the front of the board away from you, and use a G-clamp to fix one of the supports in position, flush with the lines on the edge of the leg (diagram 9).
   Drill two lead holes and fix a 30 mm (1¼ in) No. 6 screw into each hole. Repeat this exercise, fixing the other three supports to the remaining three legs.

Fitting the pot holders
23. Lean one of the sections against your work surface (with the supports towards you). Set one of the pot holders in position, with the rounded corners towards you, hard against the legs and flush with the ends of the board (see photograph). The screw holes should now lie exactly over the supports. Drill one lead hole and fix a 30 mm (1¼ in) No. 8 screw into position.

24. If you're satisfied that the holder is still correctly positioned, drill the other three lead holes and fix the screws into position.

25. Turn the section upside-down and drill a 3 mm (⅛ in) hole in the centre of the length of the pot holder at the same angle as the board so that you can drill a lead hole and secure with a 30 mm (1¼ in) No. 6 screw directly into the edge of the board. This will make the pot holders a lot stronger. Repeat this procedure for the other board.

26. Hold the two completed sections together, with the pot holders facing outwards and make sure that they are identical. If not, make adjustments now, before painting them.

Painting
27. Using a suitable wood filler, fill all the countersunk holes and, when thoroughly dry, sand off the surplus flush with the surrounding surfaces.

28. Give both sections a thorough sandpapering to smooth off rough edges and corners before applying a coat of undercoat. The two clamps that have not yet been fitted into position will also need an undercoat. When this paint is thoroughly dry, sand down both sections with fine sandpaper to get rid of any roughness on the surfaces.

29. Paint the legs and pot holders with a topcoat in the colour of your choice. You will probably have to apply two topcoats for a really good finish, but the time and effort will be well worth it. Remember to wait for each coat to dry thoroughly and then sand down with fine sandpaper before applying the next coat.

30. In the same manner as described above, give both boards and both clamps two coats of matt black paint.

Final construction
When all the paint is thoroughly dry, complete the construction.

Fitting the clamps
31. Using a G-clamp, clamp one of the matt black clamps into position, flush with the top of the board and right in the centre of the board, with the screw holes positioned nearest the top.

32. Drill right through the board, through the 4 mm (⅛ in) holes, and fit two brass bolts with their thumb screws into position. Repeat for the other board.

Fitting the sections together
33. Position the two sections together with the pot holders on the outside and, when they are flush together, use two G-clamps to hold them. When you are satisfied that the positioning is correct, fit the two steel butt hinges and remove the G-clamps (diagram 10). Using a small brush, touch up the hinges with matt black paint.

Fitting the ropes
34. Now that the two sections are hinged together, open them up on a flat surface until the feet are 600 mm (2 ft) apart. Thread the rope through the 10 mm (⅜ in) holes in the legs and tie a knot on the outside end, so that when the sections are opened out, both ropes will be under tension and the easel will stand upright.

BALANCING PARROT

This is a very popular little toy that is found in many different forms all over the world. It's easy to make and if well painted will give much pleasure to adults and children of all ages. Paint your parrot in the design and colours of your choice.

SKILL LEVEL 1

Materials

1 x 450 mm x 300 mm x 5 mm
(1 ft 6 in x 12 in x ¼ in) sheet plywood
(thickness isn't critical)
1 x 50 mm x 20 mm x 20 mm
(2 in x ¾ in x ¾ in) piece solid pine
2 fishing weights, about 100 g
(3½ oz) each
Sandpaper
Epoxy glue
Wood glue
White universal undercoat
Topcoat paint

Parrot

1. Enlarge the parrot template (diagram 1) until it measures about 400 mm (1 ft 3 in) from the top of its crest to the tip of its tail. This can be achieved either by copying the diagram freehand on to a sheet of squared paper, or by using a photocopier with an enlarging facility.

2. Transfer the outline of the parrot on to the plywood using carbon paper. With a band saw, a coping saw or a jig saw, carefully cut around the outline of the parrot. Gently smooth off the edges with fine sandpaper.

Stand

3. Draw a line at the centre of the pine (diagram 2) and square it round the width.

4. Cut a slot along this line to half the depth of the wood (that is, 10 mm [⅜ in]). This slot will need to be the same width as the thickness of the plywood you're using for the body, so that the body of the parrot will fit tightly into this stand.

Construction

5. Using a strong epoxy glue, fix one fish weight on either side of the extreme end of the parrot's tail. (Use the photograph and diagram 3 as a guide as to the positioning of the weight.)

6. When the glue is thoroughly dry, slot the body of the parrot into the stand. You will need to adjust the position of the parrot on the stand so that it balances well. Once you have achieved a balance, mark this position on the body with a pencil.

7. Remove the body from the stand and apply a little wood glue to the body; replace it on the stand in the position marked. Leave the glue to dry thoroughly.

8. Finish off by sanding the whole toy with a fine sandpaper so that there are no rough edges or surfaces.

Painting

9. Apply a coat of white undercoat to the entire assembly. When the undercoat is thoroughly dry, repeat the sanding process using a fine sandpaper, so that all the surfaces are smooth and clean.

10. You are now ready to decorate the bird in whatever colours you choose. It may be a good idea to get hold of a picture from a book or magazine and follow the design. Remember that each coat of paint must be thoroughly dry before you apply another.

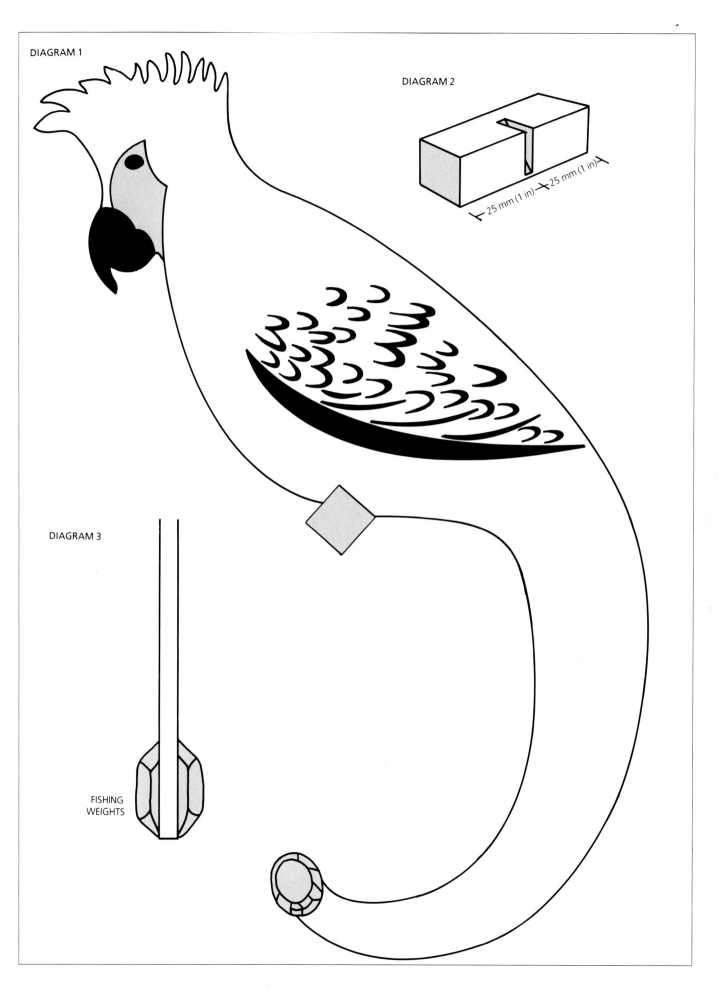

DIAGRAM 1

DIAGRAM 2

25 mm (1 in) 25 mm (1 in)

DIAGRAM 3

FISHING
WEIGHTS

MOVING DOLL

You can use your imagination on this one!
Either copy the diagrams here, design one for
yourself, or look through a children's colouring book
for ideas. It need not be a doll — it could be a
galloping horse, a jack-in-the-box, or anything else
that works on the same sort of principle.

SKILL LEVEL 1

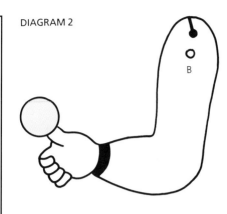

DIAGRAM 2

Materials

1 x 400 mm x 300 mm x 5 mm
  (1 ft 3 in x 12 in x ¼ in) sheet plywood
  (thickness isn't critical)
4 brass split paper fasteners
2 elastic bands approximately 7 mm
  (¼ in) long

500 mm (½ yd) of attractive coloured
  string OR twine
2 brass curtain rings OR key rings
  30 mm (1¼ in) in diameter
Sandpaper
White universal undercoat
Topcoat paint

DIAGRAM 3

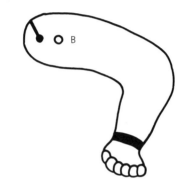

DIAGRAM 1

DIAGRAM 4

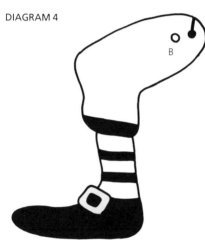

DIAGRAM 5

You can make this toy any size you wish. Either transfer diagrams 1–5 directly on to your wood using carbon paper, or enlarge them on a photocopier until the body is about 220 mm (8¾ in) long. Alternatively, the diagrams can be copied freehand on to a piece of paper, to the size of your choice.

Cutting out

1. Transfer the diagrams on to the plywood using a sheet of carbon paper.

2. With a band saw, a coping saw or a jig saw, carefully cut out the five components.

3. Drill a 4 mm (⅛ in) hole in each component at the positions marked by large dots (A & B).

4. At the dots marked B, cut in from the edge of the component to the dot, along the solid line. Using fine sandpaper, smooth off all the edges.

Painting

5. Apply a coat of undercoat to all five components. When the pieces are thoroughly dry, smooth all surfaces and edges with fine sandpaper.

6. Draw your design on the front of all the components and then paint them carefully, remembering to ensure that adjacent colours and each coat are thoroughly dry before applying the next.

Construction

7. The toy can be assembled when the paint is dry. Insert a split paper fastener through each of the four holes on the body (but not at the top of the head!). Put the appropriate arms and legs in position, pushing them on to the fasteners (diagram 6).

8. Splay the fasteners at the back. The limbs should be loose enough to move easily.

9. Slip the elastic bands into position through the slots and holes, making sure that the top one is looped through the lower one (diagram 7).

10. Attach a string and ring to the head, leaving about 100 mm (4 in) free (diagram 8).

11. Now attach a string and ring to the lower elastic band (diagram 8), so that when the lower ring is pulled, the arms and legs move up and down.

DIAGRAM 6

DIAGRAM 8

DIAGRAM 7

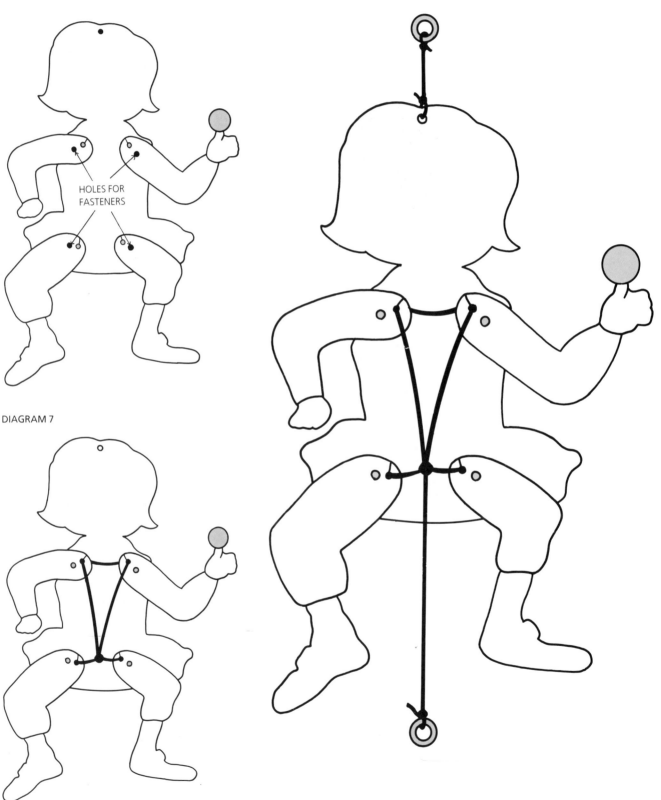

HOLES FOR FASTENERS

BIRD MOBILE

There are two ways in which this toy can be made. The first method will give you a bird like the one in the photograph, which is made from solid pine. The problem is that you really need a good band saw that can cut wood at least 110 mm (4½ in) thick. The second method uses 5 mm (¼ in) plywood. The wings and body lose their three dimensional look, but it is still an attractive toy. The instructions are for the pine mobile but can be adapted for making the plywood bird, which uses the same profiles. Construction is the same for both models.

SKILL LEVEL 2–3 (SOLID WOOD); 1–2 (PLYWOOD)

Materials

METHOD 1
1 x 1050 mm x 110 mm x 40 mm
   (3 ft 4 in x 4½ in x 1¾ in) piece pine
1 x 350 mm x 12 mm
   (13¾ in x ½ in) dowel rod
8 m (8¾ yds) nylon fishing line
2 brass curtain rings OR split key rings
1 curtain wire hook
Sandpaper
Varnish OR wood finish

METHOD 2
1 x 350 mm x 300 mm x 5 mm
   (13¾ in x 12 in x ¼ in) piece plywood
1 x 200 mm x 12 mm (8 in x ½ in)
   dowel rod
6 m (6½ yds) nylon fishing line
2 brass curtain rings
Sandpaper
Varnish OR
White universal undercoat and
Topcoat paint

Method 1
Cut the pine into three equal lengths, each measuring 350 mm (13¾ in).

Wings
1. The wing (diagrams 1 & 2) and body (diagrams 3 & 4) need to be enlarged until they are each 300 mm (12 in) long. Either draw them freehand on to squared paper, or use a photocopier with an enlarging facility.

2. Using carbon paper, copy the wing plan profile (diagram 1), on to two of the pieces of pine, making sure each time that the wing tip is at one end of the wood (diagram 5). In the same way, copy the wing side-view profile (diagram 2) on to both pieces of pine, making sure that the wing tips are at the same end, and that you *reverse* this profile on the second piece (otherwise you will end up with two identical wings instead of a pair of wings, one for each side of the bird as shown in diagram 7).

3. Draw a squared line across the wood, 300 mm (12 in) from the wing tip stub, on each side of the wood bearing a profile, as shown in diagram 5.

4. Using a band saw, and working from the wing tip inwards, cut along all the pencil lines as far as the squared line (diagram 5). When all the wing profile lines have been cut, cut across the squared line. You should now have two rough wing shapes, which form a pair, one for each side of the bird.

DIAGRAM 1

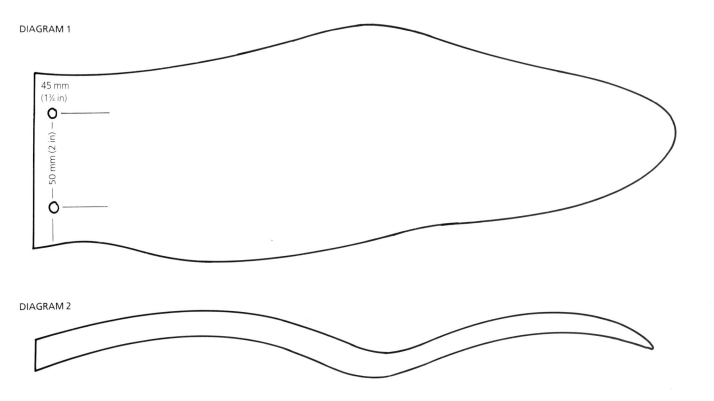

45 mm
(1¾ in)

50 mm (2 in)

DIAGRAM 2

DIAGRAM 3

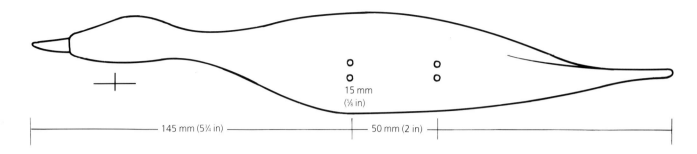

145 mm (5¾ in) 50 mm (2 in)

15 mm
(⅝ in)

DIAGRAM 4

5. Using a belt sander or a rasp, carefully round each wing at the leading edge, taper off on the trailing edge and tip until you have a realistic wing. Be careful not to taper any part too thin as it could crack under the strain of use. Try to strike a balance between realism and practicality. (Add a little detail by drawing some feathers on to the trailing edges and then filing them into shape with the edge of a rasp.) Finish off the wings to a smooth surface and edges all round with fine sandpaper.

6. Using a 2 mm (¹⁄₁₆ in) drill bit, carefully drill two holes in the stub end of each wing. These holes are marked by black dots on diagram 1.

Body
7. Cut the remaining piece of pine down its width so that you now have two pieces measuring 350 mm x 52 mm x 40 mm (13¾ in x 2⅛ in x 1¾ in).

8. As for the wings, copy diagrams 3 and 4 on to one of the pieces, making sure that the beak is at one end of the wood (diagram 6).

9. Draw a squared line across the wood 300 mm (12 in) from the tail tip on each side of the wood bearing a profile (diagram 6).

10. Cut out and shape the body, following the same instructions as for cutting out the wings, above.

11. Using a 2 mm (¹⁄₁₆ in) drill bit, drill four holes right through the body in the positions marked by dots on diagram 3.

DIAGRAM 5

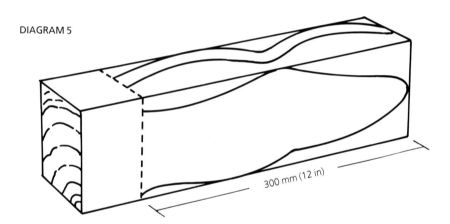

300 mm (12 in)

DIAGRAM 6

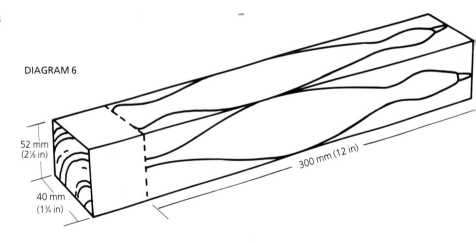

52 mm
(2⅛ in)

40 mm
(1¾ in)

300 mm (12 in)

12. In the very centre of the underside of the body, drill a 2 mm (¹⁄₁₆ in) hole to a depth of about 5 mm (¼ in), and screw the small curtain hook into this hole. Set the body aside until you are ready to begin painting.

Dowel spacer
13. Use a 2 mm (¹⁄₁₆ in) drill bit to drill a hole through the diameter of the rod, 5 mm (¼ in) from each end, making sure that the holes are parallel (diagram 9).

Painting

14. The components must be painted before construction is attempted. If you are making a pine mobile (method 1), three coats of a good varnish or wood finish will give a really good result, as the solid pine looks very attractive on its own. Paint the spacer in the same way. (Don't forget to rub down each coat with a fine sandpaper when it is thoroughly dry, before applying the next one.)

15. For best results, the plywood bird (method 2) should be painted. Apply one coat of undercoat to each component, including the spacer. With a selection of topcoat paints, finish off the bird with a realistic — or stylized — plumage. Books are a good source of ideas, unless you have a design already in mind. Paint the spacer in the colour of your choice.

Construction

It's best to construct this toy in a hanging position in order to achieve the correct balance. A beam in the garage or a high cupboard door handle will do well. The following dimensions are intended as guidelines only, as each model is likely to be slightly different, depending on how much wood has been removed in the shaping and finishing process.

Fixing the wings to the body

16. Place a piece of scrap wood or cardboard, about 5 mm (¼ in) thick, between the body and each wing, to act as a spacer.

17. Thread the fishing line through the body and wings as illustrated in diagram 7, and tie in position.

18. Remove one spacer and tie a piece of line around the two securing lines as shown in diagram 8. Repeat this on the other side of the body. The wings should now be hinged to the body of the bird.

Suspending the bird

19. Secure one curtain ring to the high fixing point. To the bottom of this ring, tie two pieces of fishing line about 600 mm (24 in) long. Tie the free end of each piece of line to one end of the dowel spacer so that the spacer is suspended (diagram 9).

20. Through each end of the dowel rod tie a length of fishing line about 150 mm (6 in) long, forming a loop. Using Plasticine or something similar, suspend the wings in the loops until the bird balances well. When you have achieved the balance, make a mark on the edge of each wing at the point where the line falls.

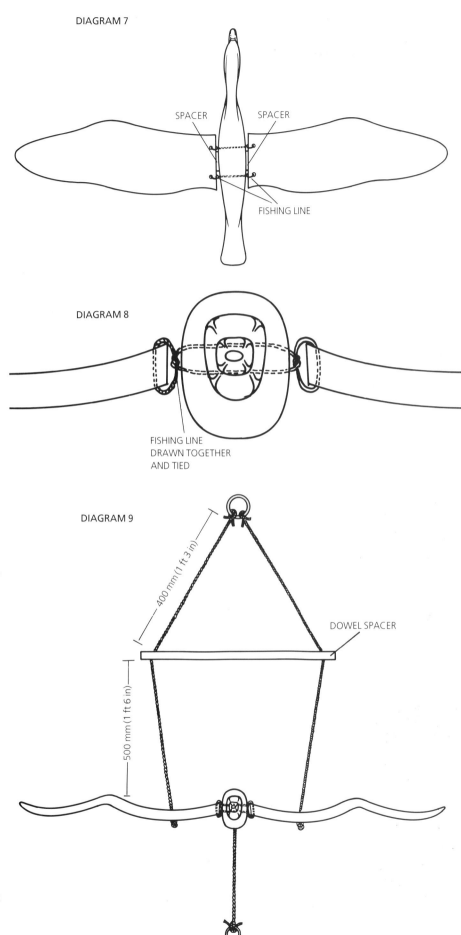

DIAGRAM 7

SPACER   SPACER

FISHING LINE

DIAGRAM 8

FISHING LINE
DRAWN TOGETHER
AND TIED

DIAGRAM 9

400 mm (1 ft 3 in)

500 mm (1 ft 6 in)

DOWEL SPACER

21. Remove the bird from the sling and drill a 3 mm (⅛ in) hole through each wing, 5 mm (¼ in) in from the mark on each wing edge. Cut the fishing line loops in the middle, so that you now have two lines that are equal in length hanging down from each end of the dowel spacer.

22. Tie each of these free ends through the appropriate hole in the wings so that the bird is suspended, balancing evenly. Tie a length of fishing line, about 250 mm (10 in) long, to the remaining curtain ring. Tie this to the hook on the underside of the body. When pulled, the bird will flap its wings.

23. When you're satisfied that the bird looks good, is balanced, and is working well, carefully cut away all the stray ends of fishing line.

Suspended from the ceiling in a child's bedroom, or over a cot, the bird mobile will provide hours of pleasure.

TWIT

This is really a very easy game to make and yet it provides hours of enjoyment, out of all proportion to the amount of time it takes to complete. It's also a wonderful idea for birthday and Christmas presents, as it costs virtually nothing and uses many of the bits and pieces of scrap wood that accumulate in the workshop. A great game for kids, it also makes for a hilarious conclusion to a dinner party!

SKILL LEVEL 1

Materials
Any scraps of wood (the greater the variety of shapes, sizes and wood types, the more attractive the set will be)
Sandpaper
Varnish OR
Univeral white undercoat and
Topcoat paint

1. Select or cut between eight and 12 pieces that are no smaller than about 100 mm (4 in) in any direction (except thickness) and no larger than 250 mm (10 in). Sand all the edges and surfaces so that each piece feels really smooth.

Finishing
2. There are two finishing options available — it's simply a matter of taste.

Varnish If the wood is a good quality hardwood, or even pine, several coats of this finish will make a very attractive set. Follow the manufacturer's instructions for applying the varnish, as different types will require different applications.

Paint Give each piece a coat of white undercoat all over. When the undercoat is thoroughly dry, apply the topcoat. You may have to apply two topcoats for a really good finish — just remember to sand down each coat to remove irregularities before applying the next. You can paint each surface a different colour if you wish.

The game
The game can be played by as few as two or as many as six players, as follows:

1. Sit in a circle with all the blocks lying randomly in the middle.

2. One player is chosen to start. This player chooses a block and places it in the middle of the playing area at whatever angle he or she chooses.

3. The player to the left of the first player selects another block and balances it on top of the first block laid down.

4. In rotation, each player selects a block and balances it on top of the growing pile. Eventually, one of the players causes the whole pile to fall over and he or she has the honour of being called, by the whole assembly at the top of their voices, *'Twit!'*

5. This twit (after recovering) re-starts the game with one block.

Players who have accumulated three 'Twit' titles are forced to retire from the game. The game continues in this fashion until only one player is left as the winner — and, of course, he or she is the biggest 'Twit' of all! Apply liberal doses of this wonderful game for relief of tension and as a remedy for shyness.

Caution: 'Twit' should not be played when suffering from a headache!

SKITTLES

Games similar to this one have provided children and adults with great entertainment for hundreds of years. Skittles is a game of skill, so the more you play, the better you'll be!
Skittles is a game that's very popular in English pubs. Adults may achieve best results by holding a pint in one hand as a counterbalance, while using the other to propel the ball.

SKILL LEVEL 1

Materials
1 x 380 mm x 380 mm x 12 mm
(15 in x 15 in x ½ in) MDF board
1 x 1600 mm x 25 mm
(5 ft 2 in x 1 in) dowel rod
1 x 500 mm x 12 mm
(1 ft 6 in x ½ in) dowel rod
1 x 500 mm (1 ft 6 in) length chain (the type used on sink plugs, although a light string will do almost as well)
1 squash ball (you can use a punctured one)
Sandpaper
Wood filler
Wood glue and strong all-purpose glue
White universal undercoat
Topcoat paint

Base
1. Draw the pencil lines on the 380 mm (15 in) square of MDF board as shown in diagram 1.

DIAGRAM 1

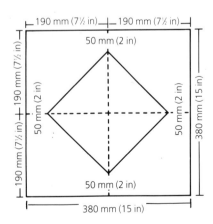

2. Draw in the points for the pins, illustrated by the large dots (diagram 2).

DIAGRAM 2

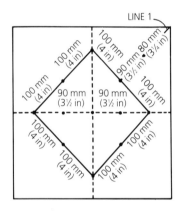

3. Then draw in line 1, and mark the dot on this line as shown on the diagram.

4. On all of the marked pencil points, with the exception of the point on line 1, drill a 26 mm (1 in) hole, 2 mm (¹⁄₁₆ in) deep. This will form the small indentation in which each pin will stand. If you have a twist bit and the point is likely to penetrate the board, don't worry, the holes on the underside can be filled with wood filler before painting. However, if you don't have this size drill bit (and it's hardly worth buying one just for this purpose), paint on a 26 mm (1 in) circle at the finishing stage. (If you are intending to paint this point on later, drill a 2 mm (¹⁄₁₆ in) hole, 2 mm (¹⁄₁₆ in) deep, at each point, otherwise these points will be lost under the paint.)

5. Drill a 12 mm (½ in) hole, 6 mm (¼ in) deep, on the pencil point marked on line 1.

Skittles
6. Cut 13 x 120 mm (4¾ in) lengths from the longer dowel rod, ensuring that the ends are square. Using a rasp and sandpaper, round off all the square edges.

Pole
7. Drill a 3 mm (⅛ in) hole, 25 mm (1 in) deep, exactly in the centre of one end of the 12 mm (½ in) dowel rod. This hole will accommodate the top of the chain. Using a rasp and sandpaper, taper this end of the pole until only a slight rim is left around the top of the hole.

Painting
8. Sand down all the components with fine sandpaper before giving them a coat of white undercoat.

9. When the undercoat is thoroughly dry, sand again before adding the top colour or colours of your choice. It looks better if the skittles and the base are different colours. You will probably find that you will need to apply two topcoats to get a really good finish. Remember that when each coat is dry, it is essential to give it a light rub down with fine sandpaper before applying another coat.

Construction
10. Fit the chain into the top of the pole, first coating 25 mm (1 in) of the chain with a strong glue. Fit the pole into position in the base — you may need to apply a little pressure. It is probably better, for both safety and storage, if the pole is not glued into place. The chain should now swing freely around the pole.

11. Drill a 2 mm (¹⁄₁₆ in) hole through the surface of the squash ball and cut the chain, so that when the free end is pushed into the squash ball, the ball will hang alongside the pole just clear of the base.

The game
The object of the game is for each player to have three 'swings' at the skittles. The ball must be swung out to the right-hand side of the pole so that it knocks down the skittles as it swings towards the player. The game can be made more sophisticated by allocating a value to each individual pin. This number can be written on the base alongside each skittle with a non-permanent felt-tip pen, or painted on permanently. As the ball knocks over the skittles, the scores can be counted.

Alternatively, each player sees how many swings it takes to knock over all the skittles and the player who uses the fewest swings is the winner.

TENPIN BOWLING

This is a good exercise for those who enjoy working on a lathe — making ten identical skittles is not as easy as it looks! If you've never worked with a lathe before, this will be a very good learning exercise. As this book concentrates on toys rather than on techniques, however, we suggest that you buy a good book on lathe work, as this will give you all the information you will need on setting up, safety and turning techniques. There are two basic groups into which lathes can be divided: the complete unit, which can be very expensive indeed; and the electric drill attachment, which is usually within the financial reach of most hobbyists. For the purpose of this tenpin bowling exercise, the electric drill attachment will be quite adequate. You will also need a set of special turning chisels; again, the cost of a basic set should not be prohibitive to the hobbyist.

SKILL LEVEL 2

Materials

1 x 300 mm x 80 mm x 4 mm
  (12 in x 3¼ in x ⅛ in) plywood
1 x 2500 mm x 75 mm x 75 mm
  (8 ft 2 in x 3 in x 3 in) hardwood
Sandpaper
Varnish OR
White universal undercoat and
Topcoat paint

Story-board

A story-board is a home-made tool that is very useful if you are doing repetitive work, especially on the lathe. It incorporates all the measurements that you will need throughout the project and prevents your having to adjust callipers and measure the same thing time and time again.

1. Cut the shape from the 4 mm (⅛ in) thick sheet of plywood and make very clear pencil points exactly as shown in diagram 1. To prevent confusion, write the measurements on it as shown on the diagram.

Skittles

2. Cut 10 x 250 mm (10 in) lengths from the 75 mm (3 in) square of hardwood. If you have a radial-arm saw or a circular saw, clamp a block to the work surface exactly 250 mm (10 in) from the blade, so that the end of the wood will lie against this stop.

This will effectively ensure that every piece is exactly the same length and prevent your having to measure ten times. This is one legitimate short cut that is worth following!

3. Clamp one piece in the bench vice and draw in the diagonals to establish the exact centre. Place a nail punch on this centre point and give it a light tap with a hammer so that it is firmly established (diagram 2).

4. Before taking the piece out of the vice, measure 20 mm (¾ in) in from each corner on each side, make a clear pencil mark, and draw in these lines across the corners (diagram 2). Repeat steps 3 & 4 on each end of the remaining nine pieces.

5. Plane away the scrap, which has been hatched in on diagram 3, so that when you turn the piece in the lathe there won't be sharp corners to turn off. These can be dangerous as they tend to either jam on the chisel or fly off in large lumps.

DIAGRAM 3

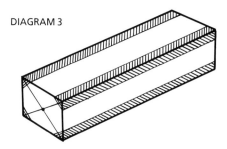

6. Set a piece in your lathe and follow these turning instructions: using your general purpose lathe tool, turn the piece down to a uniform cylinder of 63 mm (2½ in) (diagram 4). In the process of turning the piece down to the correct thickness, stop the lathe regularly and check on your progress, ensuring that you don't turn the wood more than you intend to. *Never* measure or mark the wood without stopping the lathe, as you could lose a finger or an eye. Use your story-board to measure the thickness.

7. Using your story-board, make a pencil mark on the cylinder 110 mm (4½ in) from the left-hand side (LHS). Turning the lathe by hand while resting your pencil on the chisel rest, extend the pencil mark right around the cylinder. Turn the right-hand end of the cylinder down to 45 mm (1¾ in) (diagram 5). (Use the story-board again for measuring this thickness.)

8. Using the story-board, make a mark on the wood 165 mm (6½ in) from the LHS. As before, extend the pencil mark right round the cylinder. Turn this part of the cylinder down to 35 mm (1½ in) for about 10 mm (⅜ in) either side of pencil line (diagram 6).

DIAGRAM 1 STORY-BOARD

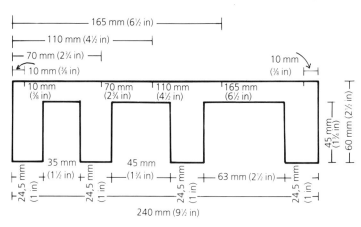

DIAGRAM 2

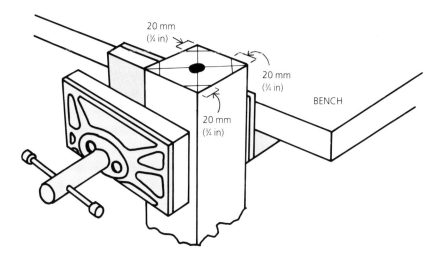

DIAGRAM 4

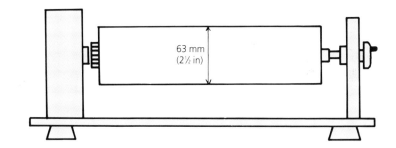

DIAGRAM 5

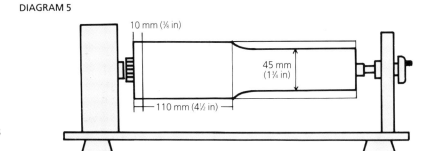

9. Turn off the 'steps' so that the shape flows smoothly (diagram 7).

10. Measure 10 mm (⅜ in) in from the right-hand side (RHS) and extend the line around the cylinder. Using a narrow, square-ended tool, turn this RHS down to 15 mm (⅝ in). You will need to use callipers set at 15 mm (⅝ in) to measure this accurately (diagram 8).

11. Using the general purpose tool, round off the right-hand end of the skittle, as illustrated in diagram 9.

12. Measure in 10 mm (⅜ in) from the LHS and extend the line round the cylinder. Using the same tool as above, turn this LHS down to 45 mm (1¾ in). Use the story-board to check accuracy. This one is important as the base of the skittle will be 45 mm (1¾ in) in diameter (diagram 9). Using the general purpose tool, round off the left-hand edge as shown (diagram 10).

13. When you're satisfied that the skittle looks as it should, switch the lathe on again and, using a fairly coarse sandpaper held gently against the skittle, sand to a smoother finish. Repeat this sanding exercise with a fine sandpaper for a really smooth finish. Remove the skittle from the lathe.

14. Repeat the steps for turning wood another nine times, until you have made ten skittles that look as similar as possible.

Hint: After you've finished the first skittle, lay it on your work bench on the far side of your lathe, so that you can keep an eye on the original while you are turning the others, ensuring that the one on the lathe shapes up like the original.

Finishing
15. When all ten skittles have been turned, use a band saw or a tenon saw to cut off the scrap flush with the base. As the base has been turned on the lathe, it will be exactly square and your skittles should be able to stand upright on a flat surface.

16. Cut off the scrap at the top of the skittle as above, leaving about 3 mm (⅛ in) on the top. Using coarse sandpaper and then finer sandpaper, round off the top of each of the skittles so that they are as smooth and round as possible.

17. Stand all the skittles in a line on your work surface. If you've done an accurate job, they will all be the same height. If there are some discrepancies, use a rasp or sandpaper to take a little off the bottom until they are uniform in height.

DIAGRAM 6

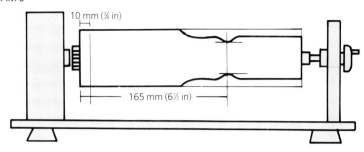

DIAGRAM 7

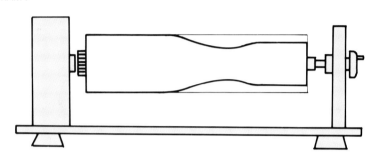

DIAGRAM 8

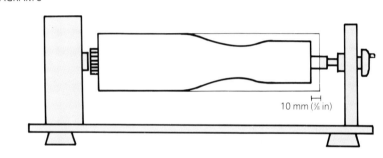

DIAGRAM 9

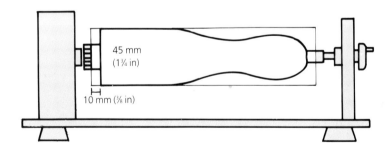

DIAGRAM 10

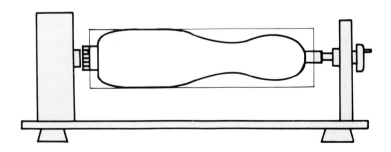

18. You may also need to use the sandpaper and rasp to adjust the diameter of the base of the skittles so that they all have a flat bottom surface that is 45 mm (1¾ in) in diameter.

Painting

As with most wooden objects, you now have the choice of either varnishing or painting your skittles. Wood-lovers will assert that, as far as possible, the beauty of wood should never be covered with paint; on the other hand, skittles are usually white. The choice is yours.

19. If varnishing, follow the manufacturer's instructions. You will probably need two or three coats for a really good finish. Remember to sand down each coat when dry, before applying another.

20. If painting, apply a coat of white undercoat to each skittle. Once this is thoroughly dry, sand down gently with fine sandpaper and apply the topcoat of your choice. You may need to apply two topcoats, or some other decoration, to achieve a really attractive finish, but the extra time will be worth the effort.

Hint: Insert a small screw into the centre of the base of each skittle before painting or varnishing. By attaching a string to this screw, you can suspend the skittle so that the whole surface can be painted at one time. The only disadvantage to this is that you will end up with a small hole in the base. This can be left as is, or filled with a little wood filler.

The game

Just about any flat surface is suitable for setting up the game, so it can be played in the garden, in the lounge, or in the hall. Place the skittles in a triangular formation, each skittle about 100 mm (4 in) from the one adjacent to it, with the apex of the triangle pointing towards the player (diagram 11). Use as much space for the bowling as you have available, adjusting it according to the age and ability of the players. Use a tennis ball for rolling along the ground at the skittles, and either play according to the official rules (obtainable from a sport shop), or make up your own rules and just count the skittles as they go down!

DIAGRAM 11

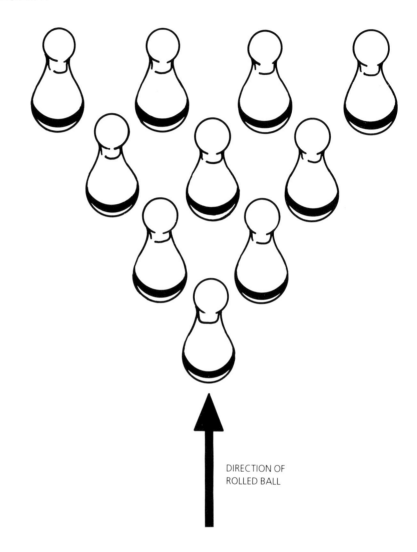

DIRECTION OF ROLLED BALL

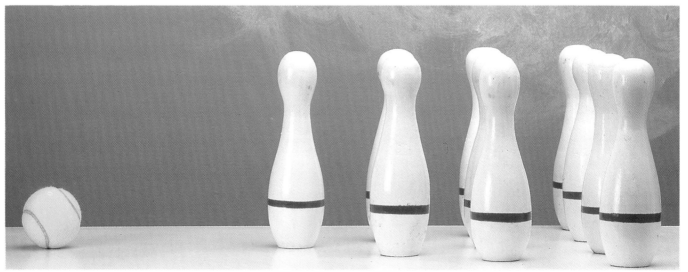

SWINGING HORSE

This variation on the rocking horse can be suspended from a tree and will provide hours of fun. It is superior to an ordinary rocking horse in that its range of movement is greater. It's also a good toy to make because very little wood is required. In fact, if you've been making other toys or furniture, there's a good chance that you'll have enough leftover bits lying around the workshop to make this toy.

SKILL LEVEL 1–2

Materials

1 x 600 mm x 200 mm x 22 mm
   (2 ft x 8 in x ⅞ in) piece pine
1 x 300 mm x 200 mm x 12 mm (12 in x
   8 in x ½ in) piece MDF board
1 x 500 mm x 25 mm (1 ft 6 in x 1 in)
   dowel rod
1 x 50 mm (2 in) No. 6 screw
6 x 40 mm (1¾ in) No. 8 countersunk
   steel screws
2 x 75 mm (3 in) No. 8 countersunk
   steel screws
9 m x 10 mm (9¾ yds x ⅜ in) nylon rope
1 x 80 mm x 4 mm (3¼ in x ⅛ in) steel bolt
2 nuts
2 washers
Sandpaper
Wood glue
Varnish OR
White universal undercoat and
Topcoat paint

Cutting the components
Main supports

1. Cut two 550 mm x 60 mm (1 ft 8 in x 2½ in) pieces from the pine (diagram 1).

2. Draw a 30 mm (1¼ in) line down the centre of the wood on one end of each support. Using a compass set to a radius of 30 mm (1¼ in), draw a semi-circle on one end (diagram 1).

3. At the other end of the wood, with your compass set at 60 mm (2½ in) (the width of the wood), draw an arc to round off this end (diagram 1).

4. Using a jig saw, a band saw or a coping saw, cut away the scrap on both pieces (indicated by hatched lines on the diagram). Using a rasp and sandpaper, smooth the ends and edges.

5. Hold both pieces together and check that they are identical — if not, then adjustments can be made at this stage. When you are satisfied that they are the same, clamp both pieces together on your work surface and, at the end shaped into a semi-circle, drill a 4 mm (⅛ in) hole through both pieces exactly at the centre.

Head

6. Using the same saw as above, cut out the head from the pine. It should measure approximately 170 mm x 190 mm (6¾ in x 7½ in). You can draw it freehand, directly on to a piece of pine. Alternatively, you can use the horse head template provided (diagram 3), enlarging it on a photocopier or on graph paper, and then transferring it on to the pine using carbon paper.

DIAGRAM 1

Neck

7. Cut a 500 mm x 60 mm (1 ft 6 in x 2½ in) piece from the pine. Round off one end, as in steps 3 & 4. Using a rasp and sandpaper, smooth the edges and corners.

8. Clamp the neck to your work surface as above, and drill two 4 mm (⅛ in) holes vertically through the neck in the positions marked by crosses on diagram 2. Countersink these holes on the top side to accommodate the head of a No. 8 screw.

9. Drill a hole the same diameter as the dowel rod, in the position marked by the large dot on diagram 2.

10. Drill a 4 mm (⅛ in) hole in the position marked with a circle (diagram 2), but do not countersink it.

11. Drill an 8 mm (⅜ in) hole in the position marked by a square (diagram 2). This will be the retainer for the rope from which the horse will swing.

Seat

12. Cut out a 300 mm x 200 mm (12 in x 8 in) rectangle from the MDF board.

13. Draw the straight lines as illustrated on diagram 4. These will be the guidelines for fitting the main supports and shaping the front of the seat. Draw one of the curved lines at the front of the seat freehand. Cut away the scrap and, using the scrap piece as a template, mark in the other curved line. This will ensure that they are the same. Then cut away this scrap, too.

DIAGRAM 2

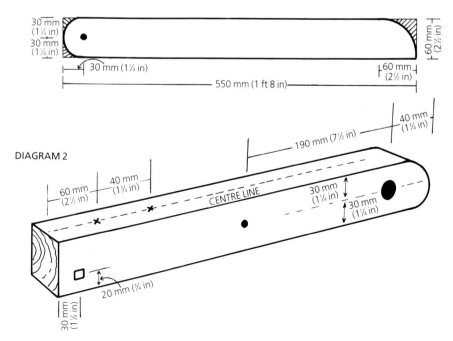

DIAGRAM 3

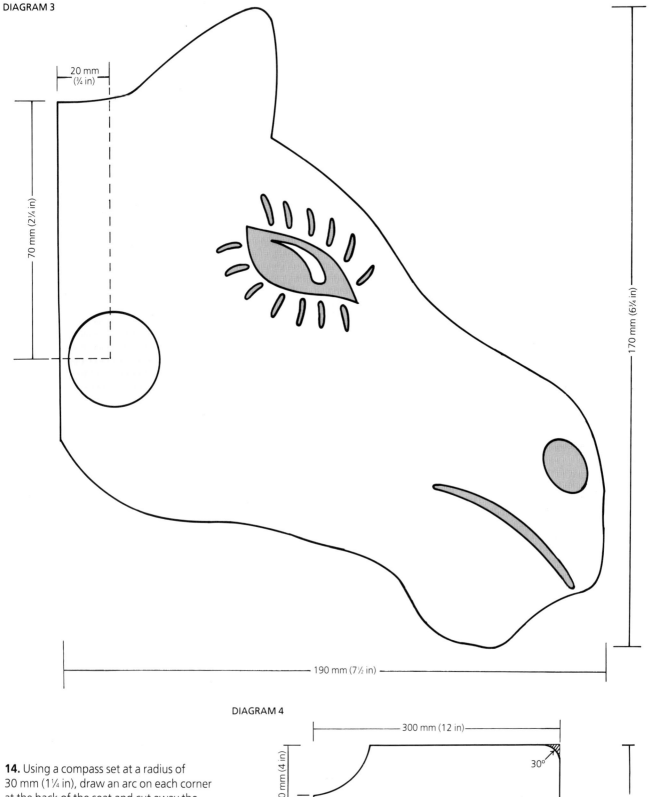

20 mm (¾ in)

70 mm (2¼ in)

170 mm (6¾ in)

190 mm (7½ in)

DIAGRAM 4

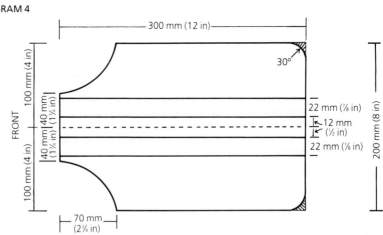

300 mm (12 in)

100 mm (4 in)

FRONT

40 mm (1½ in)

40 mm (1½ in)

100 mm (4 in)

30°

22 mm (⅞ in)

12 mm (½ in)

22 mm (⅞ in)

200 mm (8 in)

70 mm (2¾ in)

14. Using a compass set at a radius of 30 mm (1¼ in), draw an arc on each corner at the back of the seat and cut away the scrap. Using a rasp and sandpaper, or a router, round off all the corners and edges. This will be the underside.

15. Turn the seat over so that the lines you've drawn are facing downwards and drill two 8 mm (⅜ in) holes in the positions marked with black dots on diagram 5. These will be for the retaining rope.

16. Drill 4 mm (⅛ in) holes in the positions marked with crosses, and countersink them on this side (diagram 5). This will be the top.

Footrest and hand hold
17. Cut two 240 mm (9½ in) lengths from the dowel rod. Round off the ends with a rasp and sandpaper.

Construction
The horse should first be assembled without any glue so that you can make sure that

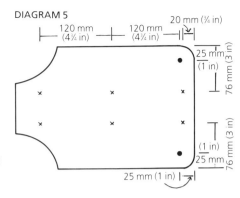

DIAGRAM 5

120 mm (4¾ in)   120 mm (4¾ in)   20 mm (¾ in)

25 mm (1 in)   76 mm (3 in)

76 mm (3 in)   25 mm

25 mm (1 in)

everything fits together correctly. Remember that for every screw there needs to be a lead hole in the receiving piece of wood. This lead hole must be the same width as the shank of the screw and the same depth as the amount that the screw protrudes through the hole in the top piece of wood.

Fitting the hand hold into place
18. Fit the hand hold into its retaining hole so that the dowel protruding on each side is exactly equal.

19. From the edge of the pine nearest to the hand hold, drill a 4 mm (⅛ in) wide hole through the pine, right through the hand hold, and into the pine at the other side, to a depth of about 10 mm (⅜ in) (diagram 3).

20. Countersink the top of this hole and, in the same hole, drill a lead hole to a total depth (from the surface) of 50 mm (2 in). Screw in a 50 mm (2 in) No. 6 screw.

21. Follow the same instructions to fit the footrest into place.

Fitting the seat to the main supports
22. Fix the seat to the two main supports with the 40 mm (1¾ in) No. 8 screws, ensuring that the supports are 25 mm (1 in) apart at the front and the back. They will therefore fit exactly into the guidelines you drew on the underside.

Fitting the head to the neck
23. Lay the head and neck on your work surface so that the top of the head is level with the square end of the neck (diagram 6).

24. Mark the position of the two screw holes on the retaining section of the horse's head using a screwdriver with a very thin blade (the line of the screws is marked by a dotted line on the diagram) and drill lead holes into the head. Fix the head to the neck with 75 mm (3 in) No. 8 screws.

DIAGRAM 6

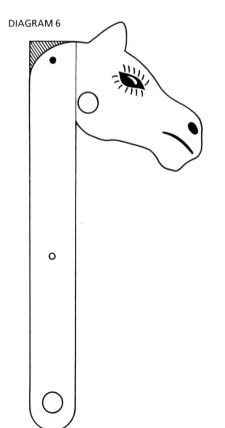

25. Draw a pencil line along the neck, and cut away the scrap, which has been hatched in on diagram 6. Drill a 8 mm (⅜ in) hole at the point marked by a dot.

Fitting the head into the main supports
26. Place the neck between the two main supports, line up the bolt hole about half-way down the neck with the bolt holes on the main supports, and push the steel bolt through, first making sure that there's a washer between the bolt head and the wood (see photograph).

27. Fit a washer to the other side, screwing on the first nut until thumb tight. This should mean that the neck will move easily between the supports.

28. Fit another nut over the first to act as a locking nut. You should now have a swinging horse that looks exactly like the one in the photograph, except for the paint and the rope.

29. When you are satisfied that everything is right, the whole job can be taken to pieces and every piece given a good sanding to ensure that it is smooth and well rounded.

30. Repeat the assembly process, this time applying a thin layer of glue to each surface to be joined.

Painting or varnishing
31. You have the choice of painting or varnishing, but remember that if the horse is going to be left outside permanently, it needs to have really good protection. Separate the neck from the supports before starting the painting or varnishing process and reassemble only when everything is thoroughly dry.

32. If using varnish, follow the manufacturer's instructions for a really good finish. This will probably mean two or three coats, with a sanding between coats.

33. If using paint, apply a coat of undercoat to the whole job. When this is thoroughly dry, sand down with fine sandpaper. Apply the topcoat of your choice. You may find that you need to apply two topcoats for a really good finish, but the extra time and effort will be well worth it. Remember to sand down each coat with fine sandpaper when it is thoroughly dry before applying the next coat.

For extra realism, add a few facial details: paint on eyes, a mouth, and nostrils in the appropriate positions, using a fine artist's brush and black paint. Make sure that the paint is completely dry before varnishing.

Finishing
34. When everything is dry, re-set the neck in the right place, making sure that the second nut is locked tightly in place. This will prevent the bolt from coming loose and causing a nasty accident.

35. Cut three 3 m (3 ft) lengths of rope, and insert one end of each of two pieces in each hole at the back of the seat. Use a figure-of-eight knot on the underside of the seat to prevent the rope from slipping through the hole (diagram 7).

DIAGRAM 7

36. Insert an end of one rope through the hole in the top of the neck section. This can either be tied in place or spliced. (Instructions for splicing a rope are too involved to include here. If you have a friend who can splice rope, make use of his or her expertise. If this is not possible, tie the rope in place with a good strong knot instead.)

When the horse is suspended in a tree, the best effect is achieved by tying the ropes at an angle away from the vertical so that the horse swings freely, as illustrated in diagram 8.

DIAGRAM 8

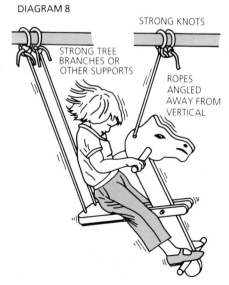

STRONG KNOTS

STRONG TREE BRANCHES OR OTHER SUPPORTS

ROPES ANGLED AWAY FROM VERTICAL

STILTS

Stilts have been a favourite among children for generations. They're very simple to make and provide children — even of four or five years old — with endless fun. One of the simple rules to remember when making stilts for children is that the younger the child, the closer to the ground the footrests have to be. The higher the footrests are from the ground, the more difficult the stilts are to balance and control; for very young children, therefore, they should elevate the child only a few centimetres off the ground. The stilts described here would probably be suitable for a four-year-old, but you can adjust the length of the handles and the height of the footrests to suit the child you have in mind.

SKILL LEVEL 1

Materials

1 x 1100 mm x 70 mm x 35 mm
  (3 ft 6 in x 2¾ in x 1½ in) piece pine
2 x 70 mm (2¾ in) No. 10 countersunk
  steel screws
Sandpaper
Wood glue
Wood filler
Stick-on shoe soles, OR a thin piece of
  rubber mat, sufficient to cut out two
  70 mm x 70 mm (2¾ in x 2¾ in) pieces

Contact adhesive
Varnish OR
White universal undercoat and
Topcoat paint

Footrests

1. Draw the two footrests on to one end of the pine to the dimensions given (diagram 1). These can be laid out together as shown in diagram 2.

DIAGRAM 1

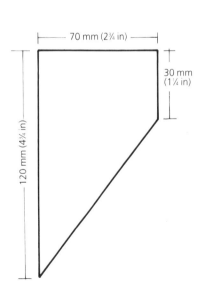

DIAGRAM 2

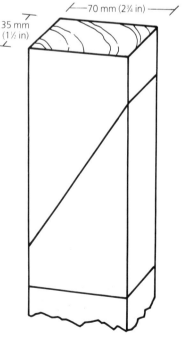

2. Using a circular saw, band saw or tenon saw, cut these two footrests out carefully. With a rasp or router, round off all the corners, with the exception of the edges on the longest side, which will fit against the handles. Finish these two pieces off with sandpaper and set aside for later.

Handles

3. From the remaining pine, cut out two handles 800 mm x 35 mm (2 ft 6 in x 1¼ in). Alternatively, you could buy ready-made handles as close to this size as possible and then attach the footrests.

4. From one end of the handle, mark two points for the retaining screws. These should be centred on the width, and at 70 mm (2¾ in), then a further 50 mm (2 in), from the end, as shown in diagram 3.

DIAGRAM 3

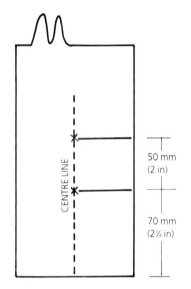

5. Using a 6 mm (¼ in) drill bit, drill the holes you have marked through the wood and countersink them on one side to accommodate the head of a No. 10 screw.

6. From the same end, but on the opposite side to the countersinking, measure 150 mm (6 in) and draw a line across. This will be the mark indicating where the top of the footrests fit on to the handles.

7. At the other end of the handle, use a rasp to shape two hand holds as shown (diagram 4). They should provide a good grip and comfortable rounded ends.

8. When you're happy with the shape of the hand holds, finish off with sandpaper. Sandpaper both handles along their full length, paying particular attention to smoothing all the corners.

DIAGRAM 4

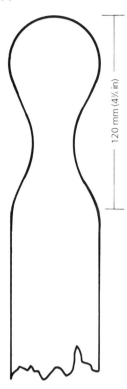

120 mm (4¾ in)

Construction

9. Now put the pieces together without glue to ensure that everything fits together well. If any adjustments are necessary, they can be made at this stage, before gluing up. The method is the same for each handle.

10. Hold the footrest in position on the handle, with the top of the footrest level with the line you drew in step 6 above, and the edges flush with the edges of the handle. A G-clamp or a sash clamp can be used to hold the footrest in position. Drill lead holes through the holes into the handle. Remember that the lead holes should be the same width as the shank of the screw, and the same depth as the length of the screw that will penetrate through the handle into the footrest. Screw in the screws.

11. When you are happy that everything is looking good and that the two parts that you have created are identical, they can be taken apart. The first two steps of construction can then be repeated; this time, apply a thin layer of wood glue to each of the surfaces to be joined. If you have decided to varnish the stilts instead of painting them, be particularly careful to wipe away any excess glue that has 'squeezed' out of the joints with a damp cloth, at this stage. If the glue is not wiped away, it will create a waterproof coating on the wood and the varnish will not take in these places leaving unsightly marks.

12. When the glue is dry, give both parts a final sandpapering to remove any rough spots. Fill the screw holes with an appropriate wood filler, and when thoroughly dry, sandpaper down so that the surfaces are flush.

Finishing

If you're going to paint the stilts, apply a coat of white universal undercoat to the whole job. When the undercoat is thoroughly dry, apply two topcoats in the colour of your choice, remembering to sand down between coats with fine sandpaper when each one is dry to remove irregularities.

14. If you're going to varnish them, you will probably need to apply three coats to get a really good finish. Remember that when each coat is dry you need to sandpaper it lightly to remove any little bumps. (Do not sandpaper the final coat!)

15. Cut two pieces from the stick-on sole, each a little larger than the bottom of the handles, which will come into contact with the ground. Apply contact adhesive to each of the surfaces to be joined (follow the manufacturer's instructions), and when the pieces are firmly stuck in place, cut away any excess with a sharp blade or craft knife.

CLOG FUN

Hours of enjoyment are tied up in this simple toy for the younger girl or boy. These clogs are easy to make, and great fun for children between about three and five years of age. They also provide an ideal opportunity to use up left-over pieces of wood.

SKILL LEVEL 1

Materials

1 x 600 mm x 100 mm x 50–80 mm
    (2 ft x 4 in x 2–3¼ in) piece pine
    (size will depend on design)
Sandpaper
A pair of old shoes the same size as the
    intended clogs OR
Stick-on shoe soles
Contact adhesive
2 m x 10 mm (2¼ yds x ⅜ in) thick
    attractive cord OR soft rope
White wood glue
White universal undercoat
Topcoat paint

Construction

1. If you have a specific child in mind, use a pair of his or her shoes as a template, or use shoes for a child of the same age. (However you decide on the size, the clogs need to be about 15 mm (⅝ in) larger than the child's foot all round.) Place the shoes on the wood and draw carefully around them.

2. Using a band saw, jig saw or coping saw, cut out the shape of both shoes (diagram 1). (If, for some reason you can get hold of only one shoe, or you have to draw one freehand, all is not lost! Cut one clog out, then turn it upside down on the remaining wood and use this shape as the template for the second clog.)

3. On the side of each clog, mark a point that is exactly half the length and half the thickness of the clog (diagram 2). (The dimensions in this diagram will not necessarily be the same as those of the clogs you want to make.)

4. Secure each clog in your bench vice and drill a hole, a little larger (10–12 mm [⅜ – ½ in]) than the cord or rope you have chosen, through the mark shown on diagram 2. It is important that this hole is at right angles to the length of the clog, and remains parallel to the thickness of the clog.

5. When you are satisfied with the clogs, use a rasp to round off the edges of the top surface of each one. Use sandpaper to finish off both clogs smoothly.

6. Paint both clogs with undercoat *Do not paint the undersides.* When the undercoat is thoroughly dry, lightly sand all surfaces to get rid of bumps and small undulations.

7. Apply a topcoat in the colour of your choice — for young children, the brighter the better! You may have to apply two topcoats to achieve a really good finish. Remember that when one coat has dried completely, you must lightly sand it before applying the next coat. To finish off the paint job nicely, you could paint the outline of a footprint on each clog in a contrasting colour.

8. Place each clog on the shoe sole that you've purchased, or taken off an old pair of shoes, to check that the size is adequate. Apply a thin layer of contact adhesive to each surface to be stuck together (follow the manufacturer's instructions) and fix the soles to the underside of each clog. Using a sharp blade or craft knife, very carefully (watch the fingers!) cut away any excess.

9. Cut the cord or rope into two equal lengths about 1 m (39 in) each, thread it through the hole in each clog and tie the ends together with a reef knot to form a continuous loop. The child holds on to this loop and pulls the cord to hold the clogs tight against his or her feet (diagram 3).

10. Apply a layer of white wood glue so that it completely surrounds the knot and immediately pull the knot into the hole in the clog; leave to dry. This operation will ensure that the knot stays fixed inside the hole, which not only improves the appearance of the toy, but ensures that the clogs function effectively, and for longer.

DIAGRAM 1

DIAGRAM 3

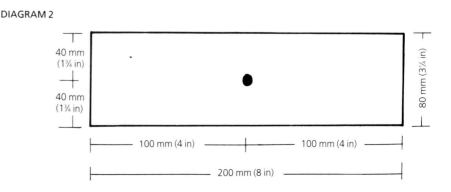

DIAGRAM 2

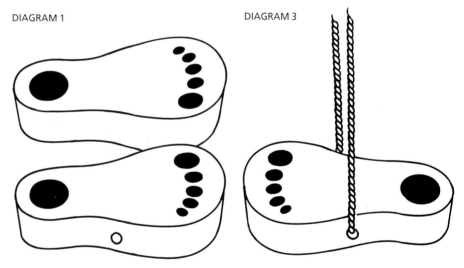

40 mm (1¾ in)

40 mm (1¾ in)

80 mm (3¼ in)

100 mm (4 in)

100 mm (4 in)

200 mm (8 in)

DUMP TRUCK

This toy looks more complicated to make than it is! It's big enough for a small child to sit in — and the tipper really works, so it can be used for moving real materials around the house or garden. But watch out that your garden doesn't get re-landscaped!

SKILL LEVEL 3

Materials

1 x 1000 mm x 300 mm x 22 mm (3 ft 3 in x 12 in x 7⁄8 in) piece pine

1 x 1250 mm x 1225 mm x 12 mm (4 ft 1 in x 4 ft x 1⁄2 in) piece MDF board

1 x 700 mm x 12 mm (2 ft 3 in x 1⁄2 in) dowel rod

Scrap of 5 mm (1⁄4 in) thick hardboard OR plywood

8 x 35 mm (1½ in) No. 10 countersunk steel screws

40 x 30 mm (1¼ in) No. 6 countersunk steel screws

16 x 35 mm (1½ in) No. 8 countersunk steel screws

1 x 20 mm (¾ in) mirror screw (with screw-in dome head)

1 x 30 mm (1¼ in) brass ring bolt

2 x 30 mm (1¼ in) steel OR brass butt hinges

Sandpaper

Wood glue

Wood filler

Wax candle

White universal undercoat

Topcoat paint

Diagram 1 will give you a good idea of the sizes of wood involved and the way in which they are laid out. However, each component section has a diagram of its own, including measurements. I have suggested that you write the name on the face side or edge of pieces as you cut them out, to avoid confusion during construction.

Main chassis

1. Using a radial-arm or cross-cut saw, cut two chassis sides measuring 610 mm x 26 mm (2 ft x 1 in) (diagram 2) from the pine and mark the face sides (which will always face outwards) and face edges (which will always be the top surfaces).

2. Now cut out four stretchers, each measuring 140 mm x 26 mm (5½ in x 1 in) as shown in diagram 3a. Use a G-clamp to hold the two chassis sides together in preparation for drilling the holes described in the following steps. (Important: the face side marks must be on the outside and the face edge marks on the top.)

3. In the chassis sides drill three 14 mm (½ in) diameter axle holes in the positions marked by crosses (diagram 2).

DIAGRAM 1

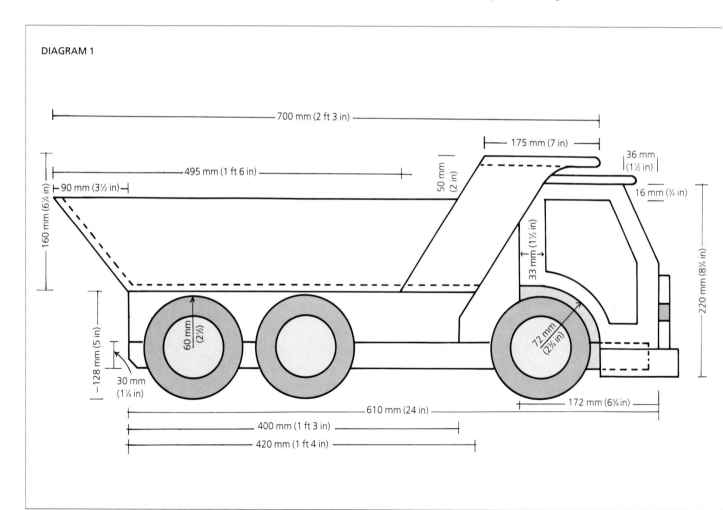

DIAGRAM 2

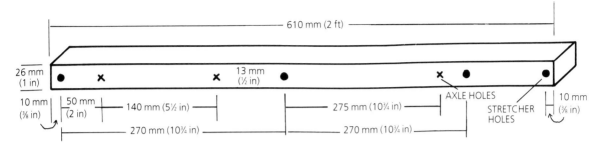

610 mm (2 ft)

26 mm (1 in)

13 mm (½ in)

10 mm (⅜ in)

50 mm (2 in)

140 mm (5½ in)

275 mm (10¾ in)

AXLE HOLES

STRETCHER HOLES

10 mm (⅜ in)

270 mm (10¾ in)

270 mm (10¾ in)

DIAGRAM 3

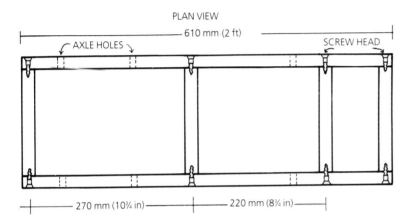

PLAN VIEW

610 mm (2 ft)

AXLE HOLES

SCREW HEAD

270 mm (10¾ in)

220 mm (8¾ in)

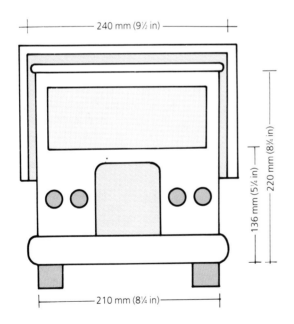

240 mm (9½ in)

220 mm (8¾ in)

136 mm (5¼ in)

210 mm (8¼ in)

4. Also in the chassis sides, drill four 5 mm (¼ in) diameter stretcher holes in the positions marked (diagram 2). The screws that will secure the stretchers to the sides will pass through these holes.

5. On the outside face sides, countersink only the stretcher holes to accommodate the screw heads.

6. Assemble these six pieces as shown in the plan view illustrated in diagram 3, using 35 mm (1½ in) No. 8 countersunk steel screws and wood glue to butt-join the pieces together.

Bin chassis
7. From the pine, cut two 420 mm x 60 mm (1 ft 4 in x 2½ in) rectangles and shape them according to diagram 4a, cutting away any scrap. Drill four 5 mm (¼ in) holes through the points marked by crosses.

8. Cut two 140 mm x 60 mm (5½ in x 2½ in) stretchers from the same pine.

9. Using the same method as in step 2, construct the bin chassis frame (diagram 4). Set aside.

Bin
Bin base
10. Before you start cutting out any of the components from the sheet of MDF board, draw the pieces on the wood, utilising as many of the straight sides of the sheet as possible. In other words, do not draw the component in the middle of the sheet and then cut into the sheet!

It makes sense to use the edges as the longest side of each component. Check the measurements and angles a second time before cutting. The first three components are each 240 mm (9½ in) wide, so you might well cut one long strip of 880 mm (2 ft 9 in), making sure that you include allowance for saw cuts, out of which you will cut three pieces. Where possible, use a radial-arm or circular saw for the cutting.

11. Cut out the base of the bin (diagram 5a) from the MDF board. Mark the face side — this will always be the top.

12. On each end mark the angles (diagram 5b shows a side view). To achieve an angle cut, draw the angle on the edge of a piece of paper using a protractor (diagram 5c). Set this angle on a bevel gauge (diagram 5d). Transfer the bevel gauge to the wood and draw in the angle on each end of the wood (diagram 5e). On the underside of the wood, draw in a line connecting these two lines (diagram 5f). Cut the angles you have just marked by setting the blade angle on your radial-arm or circular saw, or by setting the wood in your bench vice and planing down the angle using a jack plane.

DIAGRAM 4a

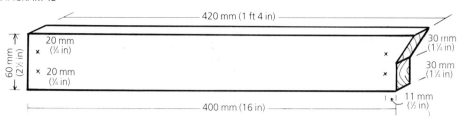

DIAGRAM 4b

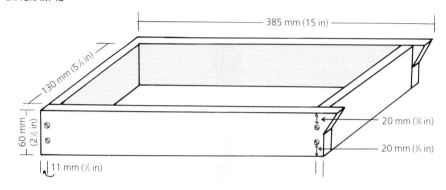

DIAGRAM 5b

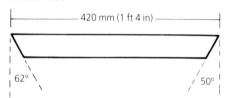

DIAGRAM 5c

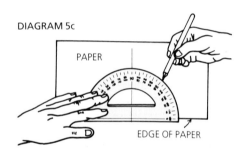

DIAGRAM 5a

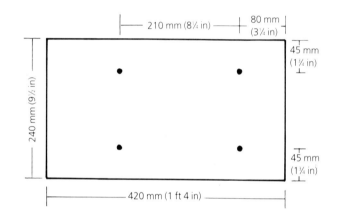

DIAGRAM 5d

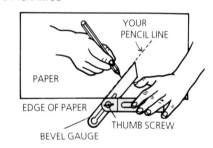

DIAGRAM 5f

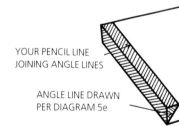

DIAGRAM 5e

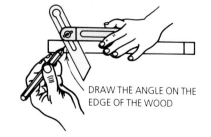

13. Drill four 5 mm (¼ in) diameter holes at the positions marked (diagram 5a), and countersink them. Write the name of this piece clearly on the face side and set it aside for later.

Bin front wall
14. Cut out the front wall from the MDF board (diagram 6a) and mark the face side — this will always be the top.

DIAGRAM 6a

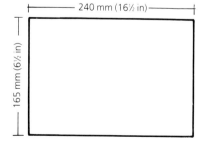

15. On each end, mark the angles (diagram 6b is an end view) and cut these angles in the same way you cut those for the bin base in step 12 above. Write the name of this piece clearly on the face side to avoid confusion at a later stage, and set it aside for the moment.

DIAGRAM 7b

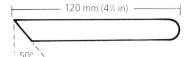

DIAGRAM 6b

Bin tail gate

16. Cut out the tail gate from the MDF board to the dimensions given in diagram 7a, and mark the face side — this will always be the top.

DIAGRAM 7a

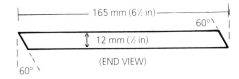

17. Following diagram 7b, which is an end view, cut one end at the given angle and round the other end using a plane or a router. Write the name of this piece on the face side to avoid confusion at a later stage, and set it aside for the moment.

Bin lid

18. Cut out the bin lid from the MDF board (diagram 8a) and mark the face side — this will always be the top. As with the tail gate, cut an angle at one end, and round the other (diagram 8b). Write the name of this component on the face side; set aside.

DIAGRAM 8a

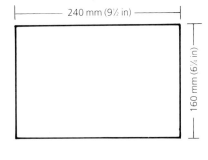

DIAGRAM 8b

Bin sides

19. Cut out one piece from the MDF board (diagram 9). The curve can be drawn freehand to your satisfaction, but make sure that it is a smooth, flowing curve. (Draw and check carefully before cutting.)

20. Place this completed piece on the MDF board and draw carefully round the outline to make a duplicate. Cut out.

21. Hold the two pieces together so that they match each other, and mark the face side on the outside of each piece.

22. Mark the screw holes (diagram 9), all of which — with the exception of those on the dotted line — are 6 mm (¼ in) from the respective edges. Drill all the holes using a 4 mm (⅛ in) drill.

23. On the face side of each of these pieces, countersink these holes sufficiently to accommodate the screw head of a 30 mm (1¼ in) No. 6 countersunk steel screw.

24. Using a rasp, round off all the edges. Set these pieces aside for later.

Driver's cab
Cab sides
25. Cut out one piece from the MDF board (diagram 10).

26. For the door space, drill a 12 mm (½ in) lead hole inside the cutting line at each edge (marked by black dots on diagram 10), then commence cutting, using a jig saw or hand coping saw. Work from each lead hole towards each corner. These edges will need finishing off with a rasp or coarse file.

DIAGRAM 9

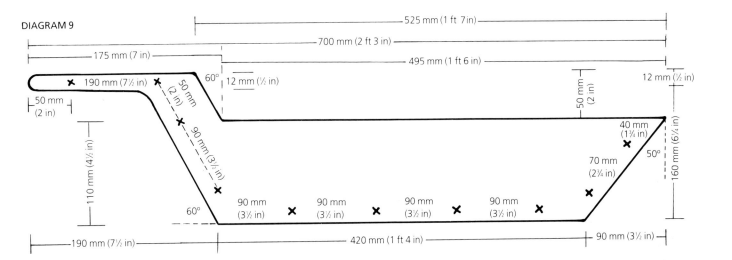

27. Repeat these steps to produce a second cab side for the driver's cab.

28. Hold the two pieces together so that they match each other and mark the face side on the outside of each piece. Mark the screw holes (diagram 10), all of which, with the exception of those on the dotted line, are 6 mm (¼ in) from the respective edges.

29. Drill all the holes using a 4 mm (⅛ in) drill. On the face side of each of these pieces, countersink these holes sufficiently to accommodate the screw head of a 30 mm (1¼ in) No. 6 countersunk steel screw.

Cab front
30. Cut this out from the MDF board (diagram 11). Mark the face side; this will always be the outside.

DIAGRAM 11

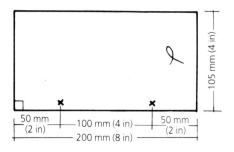

31. Drill the two screw holes (diagram 11), 6 mm (¼ in) from the edge, and countersink them from the face side. Write the name of this piece on the face side; set aside.

DIAGRAM 12a

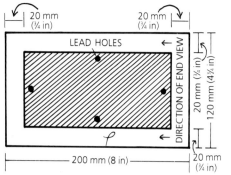

Cab windscreen
32. Cut out the cab windscreen from the MDF board (diagram 12a) using the same method as described for making the door space in the cab sides (steps 26 & 27), and cut the angles (diagram 12b).

DIAGRAM 10

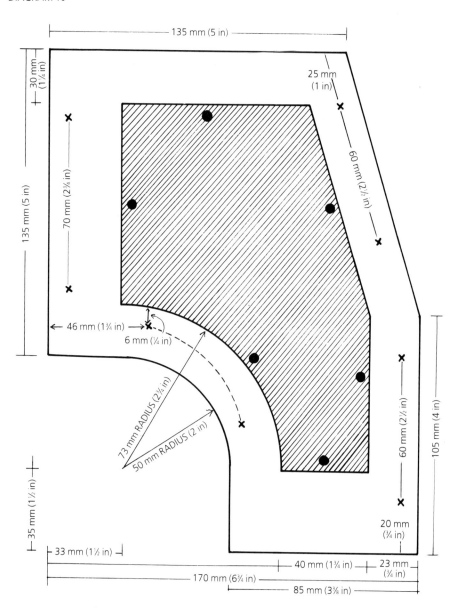

DIAGRAM 12b

Cab back
33. Cut out the cab back as illustrated in diagram 13.

34. Mark and drill two 4 mm (⅛ in) holes as marked on the diagram, and countersink these two holes.

DIAGRAM 13

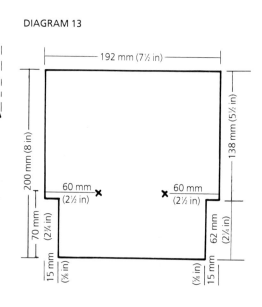

Cab seat support

35. Cut out this piece from the MDF board following diagram 14a.

DIAGRAM 14a

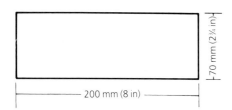

200 mm (8 in)

70 mm (2¾ in)

36. Cut the angle on the edge as shown in diagram 14b (an end view).

DIAGRAM 14b

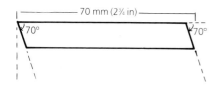

70 mm (2¾ in)

70°   70°

Cab seat

37. Cut out the cab seat from the MDF board (diagram 14c) and round the front corners to a radius of 10 mm (⅜ in).

DIAGRAM 14c

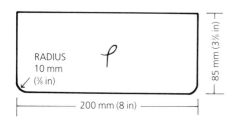

RADIUS
10 mm
(⅜ in)

200 mm (8 in)

85 mm (3⅜ in)

38. Mark the face side on the top surface of the wood — this will always be the top of the cab seat. With a rasp or router, round off the front edges and the ends. Set this aside for later.

Cab floor

39. Cut out the cab floor from the MDF board (diagram 15a), and mark the face side on the top surface — this will always be the top.

DIAGRAM 15a

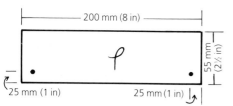

200 mm (8 in)

55 mm (2½ in)

25 mm (1 in)   25 mm (1 in)

40. Cut the angle on one of the edges, as shown in diagram 15b — an end view.

41. Mark and drill two 4 mm (⅛ in) holes on the face side, as marked (diagram 15a). These holes are measured in from the angled edge. Countersink these holes on the face side. Write the name of this piece on the face side and set it aside for later.

DIAGRAM 15b

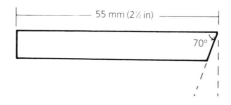

55 mm (2½ in)

70°

Cab roof

42. Cut out the cab roof from the MDF board (diagram 16) with a radial-arm saw and then cut out the curved front with a band saw or jig saw. Note that the curved front edge of the cab, which will jut out over the windscreen slightly, can be drawn freehand. Mark the face side on the top surface — this will always be the top.

DIAGRAM 16

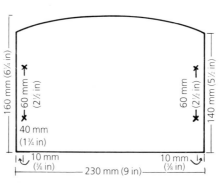

160 mm (6¼ in)

60 mm (2½ in)

40 mm (1¾ in)

60 mm (2½ in)

140 mm (5½ in)

10 mm (⅜ in)   10 mm (⅜ in)

230 mm (9 in)

43. Mark and drill four 4 mm (⅛ in) holes on the face side (diagram 16). Countersink these holes on the face side. Round off all the edges on the face side using a rasp, or a router fitted with a half-round cutter. Write the name on the face side; set aside.

Wheels

44. Using a compass, draw six circles with a radius of 60 mm (2½ in) on the pine; the centre points should be clearly visible (diagram 17a).

45. Using the smallest drill bit you have, drill a hole right through each wheel at the centre point. If you have a lathe, set a wheel in your lathe and turn the wheel so that the finished product looks like that in diagram 17b. The internal measurements are not critical and are more for decoration than any practical purpose. If you don't have a lathe, round the edges of the wheels with a rasp or sandpaper.

DIAGRAM 17a

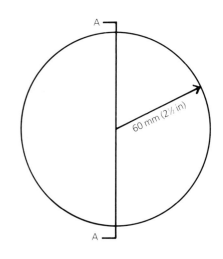

A

60 mm (2½ in)

A

DIAGRAM 17b

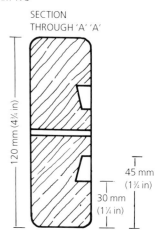

SECTION
THROUGH 'A' 'A'

120 mm (4¾ in)

45 mm (1¾ in)

30 mm (1¼ in)

46. Using a 12 mm (½ in) drill bit, drill a hole in the dead centre of each wheel, on the inside, to no more than half the thickness of the wheel. This will form the housing for the axle. Finish the wheels off by hand with sandpaper and set aside.

Axles

47. Cut three 200 mm (8 in) lengths from the 12 mm (½ in) dowel. Check that the axles fit snugly into the holes that you have drilled in the wheels. (The wheels are eventually glued on to the axles — but not yet.) Set aside for later.

Spacers

48. For the wheels to move freely, it will be necessary to make some spacers, or washers. Using a compass, draw six circles with a radius of 20 mm (¾ in) on the scrap piece of hardboard or plywood. Make sure that the centre is clearly visible. (Do not cut them out yet.) Through the centre point of each circle, drill a 14 mm (½ in) hole (through which the axle will pass). Now cut the six circles out of the board. A band saw blade might be a bit too wide for cutting these tight circles, so a hand-held fret saw will probably be better. Finish off these six discs with sandpaper and set aside.

Radiator

49. To make the radiator, cut a rectangle measuring 80 mm x 60 mm (3¼ in x 2½ in) from the MDF board and round off the corners (diagram 18). Round off the front leading edges, except the bottom edge, using a rasp and sandpaper, or your router. To make the radiator look more realistic cut some 'fins' in it. This can be achieved by drawing them at 10 mm (⅜ in) intervals and cutting with a tenon saw, or even your radial-arm saw. *Always be extremely careful when using electrical tools on such small pieces of wood.*

DIAGRAM 18

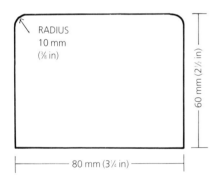

Bumper

50. For the bumper, cut out a basic rectangular shape measuring 225 mm x 30 mm (9 in x 1¼ in) from the 22 mm (⅞ in) thick pine (diagram 19). Using a tenon saw and finishing off with a rasp, round off the two front corners to a radius of 15 mm (⅝ in). Carefully cut out the scrap at the back edge of the piece (hatched on diagram 19). Shape the edges of the bumper with a rasp, or router, so that it looks more interesting and realistic than a squared piece of wood.

Headlights

51. Cut four discs with a radius of 10 mm (⅜ in) from the hardboard or plywood. Finish off with sandpaper; set aside.

DIAGRAM 19

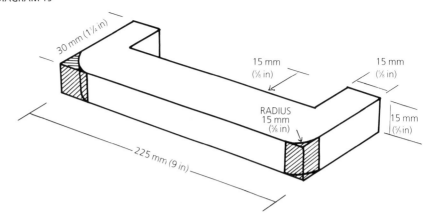

Steering column

52. Cut out the shape (diagram 20) from the remaining pine, and finish off with sandpaper. Mark the centre point of the top. This marks the position of the hole for the spindle of the steering wheel.

DIAGRAM 20

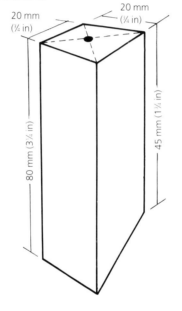

Steering wheel

53. For the steering wheel, use a small piece of scrap wood about 7 mm (¼ in) thick (or reduce a small piece of pine or MDF board to this thickness), and cut a disc with a radius of 25 mm (1 in), ensuring that the centre point of the disc is clearly visible. Through the centre, drill a 4 mm (⅜ in) hole and countersink on one side. Round off the edges thoroughly, so that the disc looks realistic, without sacrificing the thickness of the wood. This will ensure that it will stand a fair amount of rough handling.

Construction

First assemble the whole truck without glue, as detailed below, to ensure that all the pieces fit together well. If you find that there are a few minor problems with the fit, you can make adjustments at this stage.

Construction of bin

54. Place the base of the bin (diagram 5a) in a bench vice and hold one of the bin sides in place, ensuring that the face side of the side wall is on the outside, and the face side of the base is on the inside of the bin.

55. Still holding the bin side in position and using a 2 mm (⅟₁₆ in) drill bit, drill lead holes for the screw shafts through the centre of each of the screw holes on the bin side.

56. Using the 30 mm (1¼ in) No. 6 screws, screw the bin side to the base.

57. Repeat this exercise with the other side, the front wall (diagrams 6a & 6b), the tail gate (diagrams 7a & 7b) and the bin lid (diagrams 8a & 8b) until all are in the correct position. You should now have a well-constructed bin resembling the one in the photograph.

58. Fix the bin to the bin chassis, ensuring that the front edge of the chassis is level with the leading edge of the bin bottom.

Construction of driver's cab

59. Fix one side wall (diagram 10) to the cab front (diagram 11).

60. To the same side wall fix the cab windscreen (diagrams 12a & 12b). To this structure, fix the other side wall.

61. Fix the cab back in position (diagram 13); fix this structure to the front end of the main chassis, using the screw holes marked in diagram 11.

62. Fix the cab floor in place (diagrams 15a & 15b), then the seat support (diagrams 14a & 14b), the seat (diagram 14c) and the roof (diagram 16).

Fixing the wheels in place

63. Place one end of each axle into a wheel and tap on gently but firmly with a hammer.

64. Drop one of the spacers on to the axle against the wheel.

65. Place each of the axles through the appropriate axle holes on the main chassis and place one of the remaining three spacers on each axle.

66. Tap the other three wheels in place.

Placing the bin on the body

67. The bin with its chassis should fit neatly on to the main chassis, so that the back edges of the chassis are flush with each other. When the truck is finally assembled, two hinges will be secured to these edges so that the bin of the truck can be elevated. Check that the bin is clear of the cab. You now have a vehicle that looks like the one in the photograph, except for the paint.

Painting

68. If you are happy that everything fits together well, take the whole thing apart.

69. Using glue this time, reconstruct the cab and fix it to the main chassis as before.

70. At this stage, screw the steering wheel on to the steering column, leaving enough 'play' to allow the wheel to turn. Don't glue the steering column into position in the driver's side until the last stage of construction, otherwise painting the wheel, steering column and the inside of the cab will be a very tricky job.

71. First glue the bumper, then the radiator, and finally the four headlights, into position on the front of the cab.

72. Using glue, reconstruct the bin and fix it to its chassis as before.

73. Use wood filler to fill all the screw holes (and any unsightly gaps that may have appeared). When the filler has dried, use sandpaper to sand the filled holes flush with the surface of the wood.

74. Paint all the components (except the axles) with white undercoat. When the paint is thoroughly dry, lightly sand down every component.

75. Using topcoat, paint each part in the colour of your choice. You may need two topcoats to get a really good finish. Remember to sand down between each

application. This will ensure that there are no unsightly bumps or irregularities on the finished product.

Final construction

76. When all the paint is thoroughly dry, give the axles and the spacers a light rub with the candle wax, making sure that you don't get any wax on the ends of the axles. This candle wax will ensure that the wheels turn smoothly.

77. Now fix the wheels and axles in place as before, this time using a little glue on the end of each axle, ensuring that the wheels turn smoothly and are parallel to the chassis. In other words, when they turn there shouldn't be any 'wobble'.

78. Glue the steering column into position on the driver's side of the cab.

79. Place the bin on the main chassis and hinge them together at the back end with steel or brass butt hinges so that the bin can be tipped up.

80. In the centre of the bumper, screw in an attractive brass ring bolt, through which a light, brightly-coloured rope for pulling the truck along can be tied.

ROCKING HORSE

Rocking horses are a traditional favourite. They come in all shapes and sizes, from the basic model to the very sophisticated collector's piece. Here's one that's simple and inexpensive to make, looks good, is very functional and will be a treasured part of any child's toy collection.

SKILL LEVEL 1–2

4. Using a compass, draw a circle with a radius of 12 mm (½ in) (or the same diameter as the dowel rod you have for the handle) at the position marked with a cross on diagram 2.

Seat
5. For the seat, draw a rectangle measuring 350 mm x 200 mm (13¾ in x 8 in) on to your wood as described in step 3, above.

6. Draw in all the lines as indicated in diagram 3 and, using the points marked by the dots as guides, draw in the shape of the seat. Mark four crosses and two dots on the seat, in the same positions as on diagram 3.

Materials
1 x 900 mm x 440 mm x 22 mm
  (3 ft x 1 ft 4 in x ⅞ in) piece pine OR
1 x 1200 mm x 350 mm x 22 mm
  (4 ft x 13¾ in x ⅞ in) piece MDF board
1 x 240 mm x 25 mm (9½ in x 1 in)
  dowel rod
14 x 60 mm (2½ in) No. 8 countersunk
  steel screws
14 x 40 mm (1¾ in) No. 8 countersunk
  steel screws
Sandpaper
Wood glue
Wood filler
Varnish

Cutting the components
1. Draw the components on the pine or MDF board first, to ensure best usage and least wastage. Leave all the cutting out until you're satisfied that you've used the available wood to the best advantage.

Supports
2. Draw two pieces following diagram 1, but draw the curved bottom on one piece only. When you've cut that one out it can be used as a template from which to draw the other; this will ensure that they are as similar as possible.

Head
3. Draw a 300 mm x 240 mm (12 in x 9½ in) rectangle on your wood, using one edge of the wood and a square to ensure that the rectangle has 90° corners. Draw the head of a horse within this rectangle. Even if you're not artistic, this won't be as difficult as it sounds. Find a good profile picture of a horse's head (I took mine from a children's encyclopaedia) and, using a soft pencil, lightly draw in the lines, making alterations as you go along. If that's a total failure, enlarge diagram 2 on a photocopier until it fits the rectangle, and then use carbon paper to trace the shape on to your wood.

DIAGRAM 1

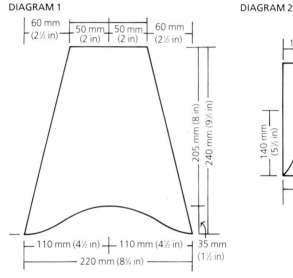

DIAGRAM 2

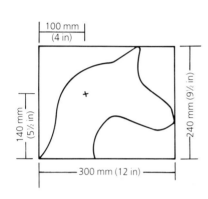

DIAGRAM 3

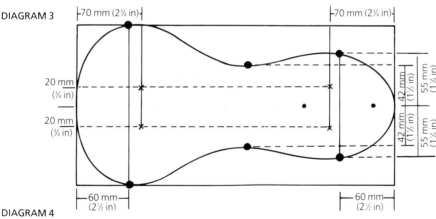

DIAGRAM 4

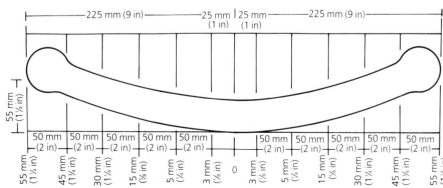

Rockers

7. Draw one of the rockers on to the wood, following diagram 4. When you have cut this one out satisfactorily, you can use it as a template for the other, so that they will be as similar as possible.

8. Using a band saw, jig saw or coping saw, cut out the first support, on which you have drawn the curved bottom, and place it on top of the other support, which you've only partially drawn. Draw round the bottom of the first support to produce an accurate curve for the second support. Cut out the second support.

9. Cut out the rocker that you've drawn and, using a rasp and sandpaper, or a belt sander, smooth off all the edges so that all the curves are smooth and rounded. When you're satisfied with the shape of this rocker, place it on a clear piece of wood and, using it as a template, draw around it and cut out the second rocker.

10. Clamp them together with a G-clamp and then on to your work surface or in your bench vice. Using a rasp and sandpaper, round off the edges of the rockers. Remember to keep the edges square (diagram 5).

DIAGRAM 5

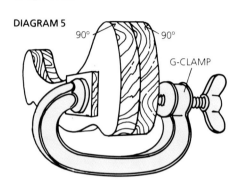

11. Cut out the seat. Set a bevel gauge to an angle of 15° and place it alongside the seat. Now drill a 4 mm (⅛ in) hole at each of the crosses, 15° away from the vertical

(diagram 6). If you're not sure how to achieve an angle of 15°, refer to step 12 on page 74 for more information.

12. Drill a vertical 4 mm (⅛ in) hole at the points marked with a dot (diagram 3); countersink them on the underside.

DIAGRAM 6

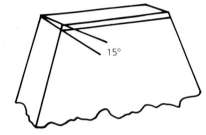

13. Cut out the head as drawn and drill a 25 mm (1 in) hole at the point marked (diagram 2). This will accommodate the handle. If you don't have a 25 mm (1 in) drill bit, you can drill a lead hole inside the circle

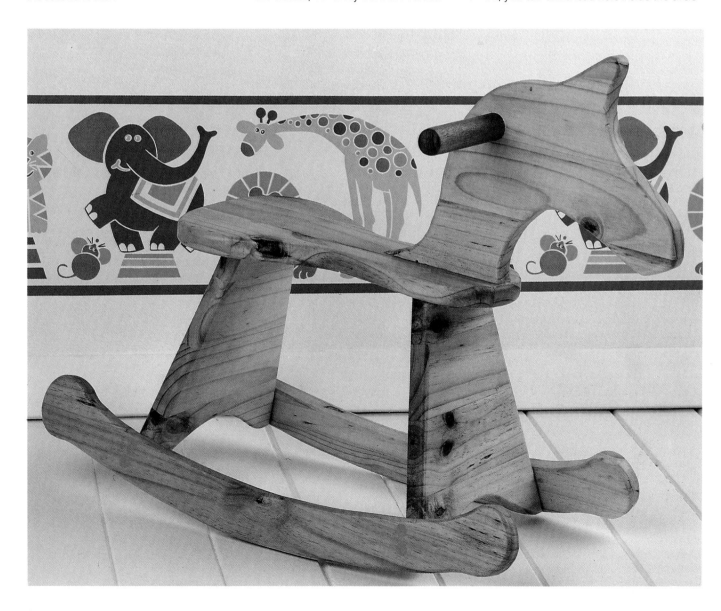

and cut around the circle with a jig saw or pad (keyhole) saw. Remember that the lead hole will have to be wider than the width of the blade you will use.

Finishing the components

14. The supports need to be at an angle to the seat so, using the bevel gauge (still set at 15°) and following diagram 6, mark a 15° angle on each top edge and join the lines along the side as shown (diagram 6).

DIAGRAM 7

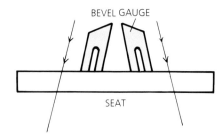

BEVEL GAUGE

SEAT

Using either a radial-arm saw or circular saw set at 15°, cut away the scrap. If you do not have such a saw, plane away the scrap.

15. Using a rasp and sandpaper, or a router, round off the edges on all the pieces except the straight edge on the bottom of the head and that at the top of the supports.

Construction

The horse should first be assembled without any glue, to ensure that all components fit together well. Remember that all screws will need a lead hole in the receiving piece of wood. This hole should be the same width as the shank of the screw you are using, and as deep as the length of screw that will protrude from the hole in the piece of wood being joined to the receiving piece.

Fitting the seat to the supports

16. First fix one of the supports in your bench vice and hold the seat in place, making sure that the support will be angled in the right direction. Ensuring that the support is in the centre of the seat and that the line of the screw holes is in the centre of the support, drill one lead hole and screw in one of the 60 mm (2½ in) screws. Check that the seat is still in exactly the right position, then drill the other lead hole and screw in another screw. Repeat for the other support.

Fitting the head to the seat

17. Put the head in your bench vice with the straight edge uppermost and parallel to the top of your work surface. Hold the seat in position, making sure that the front edge of the head is flush with the front of the seat, and that the head is exactly in the centre of

DIAGRAM 8

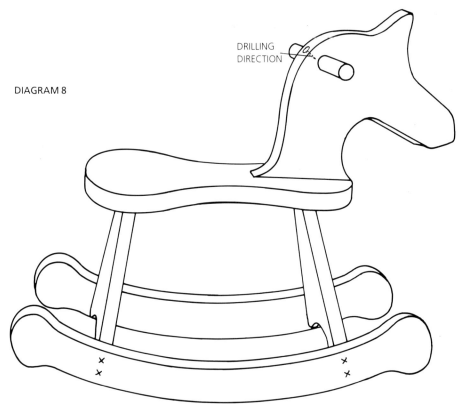

DRILLING DIRECTION

the seat. Drill one lead hole and secure one of the 60 mm (2½ in) screws. Check that the head is still flush and centred before drilling the second lead hole and securing a screw.

Fitting the rockers

18. Lay the horse on its side on the work surface and hold one rocker in position so that the overlap on each end is the same and so that there is a clearance of 10 mm (⅜ in) between the bottom of the rocker and the bottom of the support (diagram 8). Mark the position of the four screw holes to be drilled, indicated by crosses on diagram 8.

19. Remove the rocker and place it on your work surface. Drill four 4 mm (⅛ in) holes at the crosses and countersink these. Replace the rocker on the support and drill one lead hole and screw in one of the 40 mm (1¾ in) screws. If you're satisfied that the rocker is still in the correct position, drill the other three lead holes and screw in the screws. Repeat for the other rocker.

Fitting the handle

20. Push the handle through its retaining hole until the overlap on each side of the head is exactly equal. Drill a 4 mm (⅛ in) hole through the edge of the head, from the position nearest the handle. Drill straight through the handle and into the wood on the other side — about 10 mm (⅜ in). The direction and position of the drilling is marked on diagram 8 by the dotted line. Countersink this hole, and drill a lead hole

through it for the 60 mm (2½ in) screw. Screw into position. Your rocking horse should now look like the one in the photograph.

Finishing

21. When you're satisfied with the result, take the horse to pieces and give every component a good sanding with fine sandpaper so that there are no pencil marks or rough edges and corners.

22. Follow the assembly steps above, but this time spread a thin layer of suitable wood glue on the surfaces to be joined.

23. Using wood filler as near in colour to the natural colour as possible, fill all the countersunk holes. When this filler is thoroughly dry, sandpaper the filler flush with the surrounding surface.

Painting and varnishing

This horse looks very good finished off with varnish, but you can paint it if you prefer.

24. If varnishing, you could add a couple of details such as eyes and a mouth. These can be drawn either with a felt-tip pen, or carefully painted using a fine artist's brush and black paint, preferably before applying the varnish.

25. Apply three coats of your chosen varnish, remembering to use light sandpaper between each coat.

MONKEY SWING

This is definitely the easiest toy to make in the whole book, yet it provides endless hours of fun for children of all ages.

SKILL LEVEL 1

Materials

1 x 300 mm x 300 mm x 22 mm piece pine (12 in x 12 in x ⅞ in) (thickness isn't critical, but shouldn't be thinner than 22 mm [⅞ in] for safety's sake)
3 m x 10 mm (3¼ yds x ⅜ in) nylon rope
Sandpaper
Varnish OR
Wood sealer
White universal undercoat
Topcoat paint
A convenient tree, with a strong branch about 3 m (3¼ yds) off the ground!

Construction

1. Establish the centre of the 300 mm x 300 mm (12 in x 12 in) pine by drawing two diagonal lines across it (diagram 1).

DIAGRAM 1

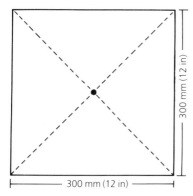

300 mm (12 in)

300 mm (12 in)

DIAGRAM 2

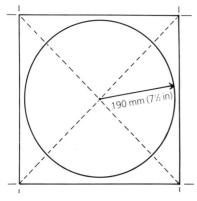

190 mm (7½ in)

2. Using a compass set to a radius of 140 mm (5½ in) (which is about the limit of an ordinary compass), draw a circle on the wood (diagram 2).

3. Drill a 10 mm (⅜ in) hole through the board at the exact centre point. Cut around the outside of the circle with a jig saw, band saw or coping saw and, using a router or a rasp and sandpaper, round off all the edges (diagram 3).

DIAGRAM 3

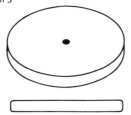

4. Smooth the disc with fine sandpaper.

Varnishing

5. If the pine is an attractive piece of wood, use a good exterior quality varnish or wood sealer, following the manufacturer's instructions carefully. You will probably need to apply three or four coats to achieve a really satisfactory and durable finish. Do not skimp on the finishing because wood exposed to the elements all year round doesn't last very long.

Painting

6. If you are painting your swing, give the whole disc a coat of undercoat and sand down when thoroughly dry.

7. Apply the topcoat of your choice. You will probably have to apply two topcoats to achieve a really good finish, but the extra time and effort will be well worth it. Remember to sand down each coat when thoroughly dry, before applying the next.

Finishing

8. Insert one end of the rope through the centre hole and tie a thick knot on the underside of the swing (diagram 4). The figure-of-eight, which is the knot used by sailors to prevent the end of a rope from slipping free through a fairlead, is a good knot to use for this purpose.

DIAGRAM 4

9. Attach the other end of the rope very securely to a tree branch, or other convenient fixing point, so that the seat is about 300 mm (12 in) off the ground — and get the kids swinging!

FORT

This project is graded skill-level 2 and may look quite complicated, but it is basically an exercise in accurate measuring and cutting. Have a go, because it's really quite straightforward!

SKILL LEVEL 2

Materials

1 x 1500 mm x 900 mm x 12 mm
  (5 ft x 3 ft x ½ in) MDF board
1 x 650 mm x 10 mm (2 ft 1 in x ⅜ in)
  dowel rod
80 x 30 mm (1¼ in) No. 6 countersunk
  steel screws
2 x 20 mm (¾ in) brass or steel butt
  hinges and screws
2 small chains (for effect)
Sandpaper
Wood glue
White universal undercoat
Topcoat paint

Cutting plan

The purpose of using the cutting plan is to achieve maximum efficiency. The best way to use a sheet of MDF board of this size is shown on the cutting plan below.

1. Copy the cutting plan on to your sheet of MDF board to make sure that there's enough wood for the job. After drawing in the rectangular shapes, draw in the individual details following the rest of the instructions, before carefully cutting them away from the sheet. This will save some duplication of instructions.

Cutting out

The best method of cutting out the major pieces will be by using a radial-arm or circular saw. Alternatively, a hand-held circular saw, an electric jig saw, or even a cross-cut hand saw will do the job very well. Cut slowly, carefully and as accurately as you can. To avoid later confusion when the fort is constructed, write the name on each piece after you've cut it out.

Base

2. Cut out the base as shown in diagram 1 and mark the top side with a face mark. Drill the 4 mm (⅛ in) holes (diagram 1) and countersink all of them on the underside.

Walls and battlements

3. The method used for cutting out all the walls and the battlements is the same. Draw the piece accurately on the board, including the battlement details and other 'holes'. Cut out the main rectangle (that is, right around the outside measurements).

4. Cut out any doors, battlements and other 'holes' with a band saw, coping saw or jig saw. Four cuts should effectively take out scrap (diagram 2).

CUTTING PLAN

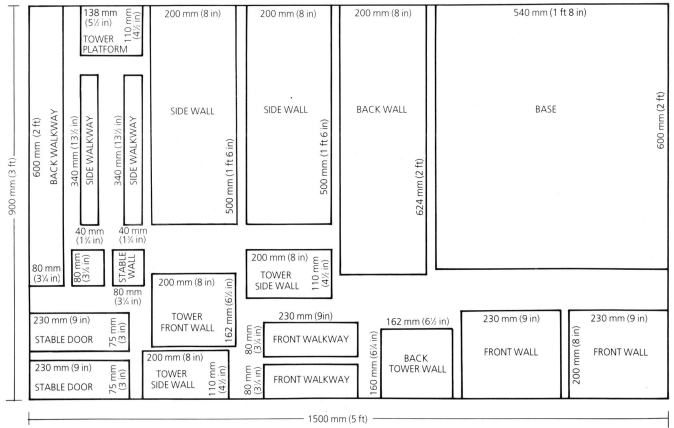

DIAGRAM 1

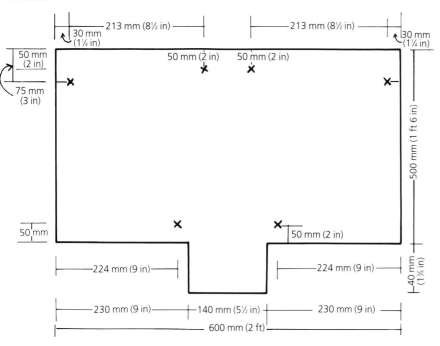

6. On the inside, draw a line 40 mm (1¾ in) from, and parallel to, the bottom edge. This marks the floor level of the fort and the line against which the base will fit.

7. Also on the inside, draw a line 60 mm (2½ in) from, and parallel to, the top edge. This marks the top of the walkway.

Side walls
8. Prepare two pieces for the side walls, following all the instructions above, but using the dimensions shown in diagram 3.

Front walls
9. Repeat these steps for the front wall, using the dimensions shown in diagram 5. You will need two pieces of this size.

Tower front
10. Prepare the tower front piece as shown in diagram 6, including the two lines on the inside, as for the back wall (steps 6 & 7).

11. Drill four lead holes in the positions indicated by the black dots. The diameter of the holes must be greater than the width of the saw blade you will use. Now cut out the door space using a keyhole saw or jig saw.

DIAGRAM 2

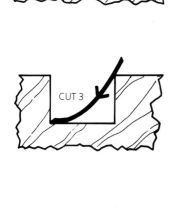

Back wall
5. Draw, cut out and drill and countersink holes for the back wall (diagram 4). This side will be the outside.

DIAGRAM 3

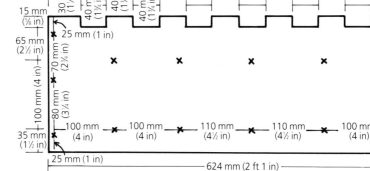

DIAGRAM 5

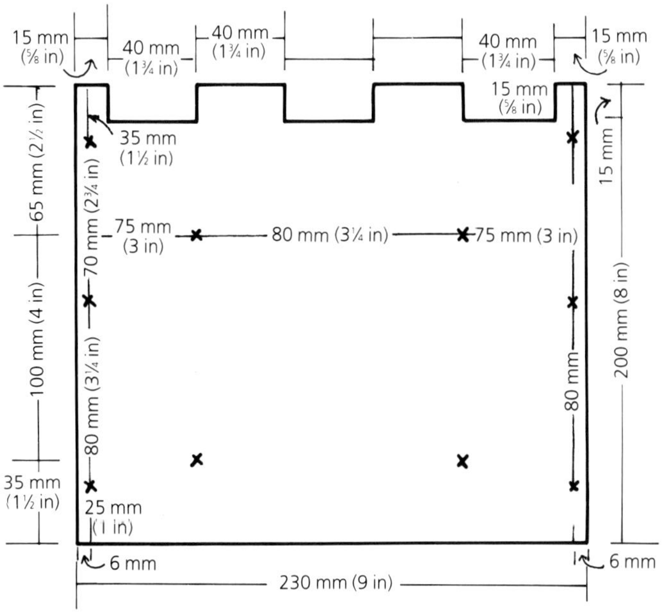

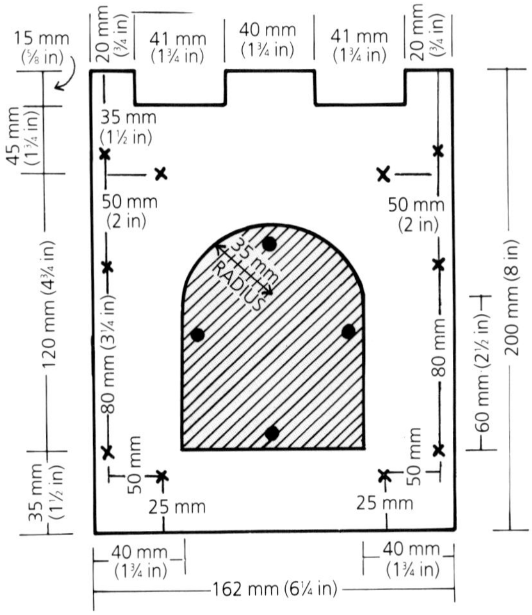

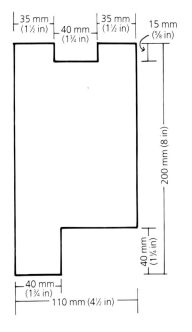

Tower sides
12. Prepare two tower sides (diagram 7).

Tower back
13. Prepare a tower back piece (diagram 8).

Tower roof
14. Cut a rectangle for the tower roof as shown (diagram 9). Draw in the diagonals to establish the centre point.

15. Drill a hole 10 mm (⅜ in) in diameter on this centre point, but to only half the thickness of the wood. This will form the seat for the flag-pole.

DIAGRAM 9

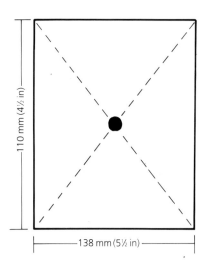

DIAGRAM 6

Drawbridge
16. Cut out a rectangle measuring 100 mm x 90 mm (4 in x 3½ in); diagram 10 is a side view of the rectangle you've just cut.

DIAGRAM 7

DIAGRAM 8

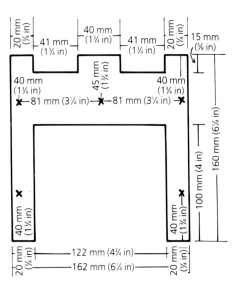

DIAGRAM 10

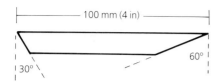

100 mm (4 in)

30°   60°

17. Using a bevel gauge that you have set from a protractor, mark the angles on the sides of the wood. (See step 12 on page 74.) With a piece of wood as small as this, perhaps the best way of cutting these two angles is to draw lines across the underside of the wood at the appropriate place (connecting the lines you drew on the sides), secure the wood in your bench vice, or G-clamp it to the top of your work surface, and plane away the scrap.

Walkways
18. Cut two rectangles measuring 340 mm x 40 mm (13½ in x 1¾ in).

19. Cut one rectangle measuring 600 mm x 80 mm (2 ft x 3¼ in) and drill six 4 mm (⅛ in) holes as shown (diagram 11) and countersink them on the top side. This piece will be the walkway against the back wall.

DIAGRAM 11

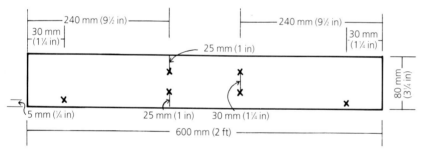

240 mm (9½ in)   240 mm (9½ in)
30 mm (1¼ in)   30 mm (1¼ in)
25 mm (1 in)
80 mm (3¼ in)
5 mm (¼ in)   25 mm (1 in)   30 mm (1¼ in)
600 mm (2 ft)

20. Cut two rectangles measuring 230 mm x 80 mm (9 in x 3¼ in) for the walkways at the front wall of the fort.

Walkway supports
21. Cut two rectangles measuring 85 mm x 80 mm (3⅜ in x 3¼ in).

Doors
22. Cut two rectangles measuring 230 mm x 85 mm (9 in x 3⅜ in).

Construction
You are now ready to begin construction. Remember that when the pieces are held in place, there needs to be a lead hole for each screw — in the case of a No. 6 screw, a 2 mm (1/16 in) drill bit should be suitable. The fort should first be assembled without any glue, to ensure that all the pieces fit together well. If any adjustments are necessary they can be made at this stage.

23. Clamp the base to your work surface with one of the sides protruding over the edge. Hold one of the side pieces in position (with the ends flush with the ends of the base and with the countersinking on the outside) and drill a lead hole into the base through a hole at one end.

24. Screw one of the 30 mm (1¼ in) No. 6 screws into this hole, but not very tightly.

25. Repeat this procedure at the other end, and when you are satisfied that the side piece is flush with the ends, drill lead holes and screw in the remaining screws.

26. Following the same procedure as above, fix the opposite side into position.

27. Now fix the back wall into position.

28. Follow up by fixing the front wall, the side walls and the back wall of the tower into position.

29. Fix on the roof of the tower.

30. Now fix the two front walls of the fort into position.

31. Fix the back walkway, and the front and side walkways into position.

32. Fix the two supports into position. At this stage, set aside.

Prison
33. Cut a small rectangular retaining bar from a scrap of MDF board and, using a rasp and sandpaper, round off the ends as shown (diagram 12).

DIAGRAM 13

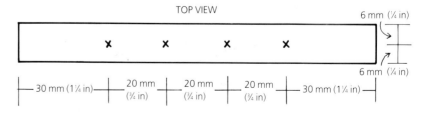

TOP VIEW

6 mm (¼ in)

6 mm (¼ in)

30 mm (1¼ in)   20 mm (¾ in)   20 mm (¾ in)   20 mm (¾ in)   30 mm (1¼ in)

DIAGRAM 12

120 mm (4¾ in)
SIDE VIEW

34. Draw four evenly spaced marks on the top of this retaining bar, in the centre of the piece (diagram 13). Write 'front' on the front side to avoid confusion later.

35. Using a G-clamp, fix the retaining bar to the back walkway, in the exact centre of the two supports, and flush with the front edge of the walkway.

36. Drill the holes you have marked through the retaining bar and the walkway, using a drill bit as thick as the dowel to be used.

37. Separate the retaining bar from the walkway and, using a drill bit 2 mm (1/16 in) thicker than the holes you have just drilled, enlarge the holes in the walkway. This will allow the prison bars to move up and down smoothly.

38. Cut four 115 mm (4⅜ in) lengths of dowel rod and, using sandpaper, round one end of each. Insert the square ends of the dowel rods into the retaining bar and (keeping the front towards you) insert the bars. The bottom ends of the prison bars should just touch the floor of the fort and the retaining bar should sit snugly on top of the walkway. Adjust the bars in their holes until this is achieved.

Fitting the doors
39. Hold one of the doors in position, with its inside edge 2 mm (1/16 in) away from the support; drill a lead hole into the top of the door through the hole in the walkway. Screw into place, but not too tightly.

40. From the underside of the fort, drill a lead hole into the bottom of the door and screw into place. By adjusting the top and bottom screw of the door, you will be able to make the door swing, as if on hinges. Repeat this for the other door.

Fitting the drawbridge

41. Stand the fort on its back wall with the entrance door at the top and lay the drawbridge in the exact centre of the tower, covering the entrance. Use the two hinges to join the drawbridge to the front wall of the tower (diagram 14). With the fort in the upright position, the drawbridge should hinge up and down. Two small chains can be added for effect later.

Flag-pole

42. Cut a 150 mm (6 in) length of 10 mm (⅜ in) dowel and gently round one end of

DIAGRAM 14

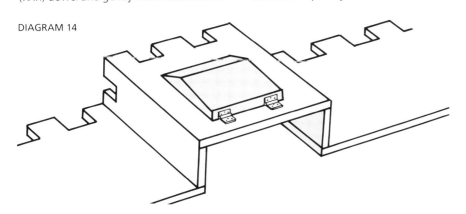

the dowel with sandpaper. Insert the square end of the dowel into the retaining hole in the roof of the tower. You should now have a fort that looks like the one in the photograph, except for the painting.

43. When you are satisfied that everything fits together well and that everything is working as it should, the whole project can be taken to pieces. Now construct the fort as above, but this time use a light, smooth coat of wood glue on each surface to be joined permanently together. Do not put the doors in place yet.

Painting

44. Using wood filler, go over the entire fort, filling all the countersunk holes, except those for the drawbridge hinges. When this is dry, use sandpaper to bring the fillings flush with the adjacent surfaces.

45. Paint the fort and the doors, prison bars, drawbridge and flag-pole with undercoat. When the undercoat is dry, smooth off all surfaces with a light sandpaper.

46. Apply one or two topcoats in a colour of your choice. Sand each coat when dry before applying the next.

Finishing off

47. Fit the two doors into position.

48. Push the flag-pole into position. Do not glue it as it could easily be broken, leaving a dangerous spike protruding from the top of the tower. It will be far safer having the flag-pole fitted into position and secured with a little adhesive putty.

49. Drop the prison bars into place. Add a smart, personalized flag to the flag-pole.

KITCHEN STOVE

Every child loves to 'cook', and this little stove provides the ideal opportunity. As children's pots, pans and utensils are obtainable from most good toy stores, a stove can become the basis for a whole collection of toys.

SKILL LEVEL 2–3

Materials

1 x 1500 mm x 900 mm x 12 mm
   (5 ft x 3 ft x ½ in) sheet MDF board
1 x 400 mm x 350 mm x 4 mm
   (1 ft 3 in x 13¾ in x ⅛ in) sheet plywood
1 x 280 mm x 245 mm x 3 mm
   (11 in x 9¾ in x ⅛ in) sheet Perspex
24 x 30 mm (1¼ in) No. 6 steel
   countersunk screws
2 x 40 mm (1¾ in) steel or brass butt
   hinges or a piano hinge about
   200 mm (8 in) in length
3 OR 4 panel pins
1 m (1 yd) chain with links
   approximately 10 mm (⅜ in)
1 magnetic cupboard door catch
4 plastic screw-top bottle lids
2 drawer handles (see photograph)
Sandpaper
Wood glue
Wood filler
Wax candle
White universal undercoat
Topcoat paint
Matt black paint

Cutting out components

You will use the same method for cutting out most of the main components, so only simple instructions and a diagram showing dimensions are given. Detailed instructions are not given for each stage.

As far as possible, all cutting should be done with a circular saw, either as a table saw or a radial-arm saw. A jig saw will be useful for cutting into corners.

The sheet of MDF board that you buy is factory produced, so you should be able to rely on the corner angles being square — but it's worth checking! Working from the edges of the bought board will ensure accuracy and maximum use of the board.

On each diagram, the screw holes to be drilled are marked and their positions are given. If the screw is close to an edge, it must be assumed that it is 6 mm (¼ in) from this edge, unless otherwise specified. Each screw hole should be 4 mm (⅛ in) in

diameter and countersunk on one side only (always the outside), to accommodate the head of a No. 6 screw.

Stove back

1. Cut out a rectangle to the dimensions given and drill the screw holes as indicated (diagram 1). (It will be easiest to cut out the full rectangle before cutting out the two small side pieces.)

DIAGRAM 1

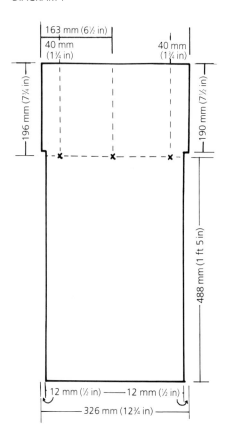

Stove sides

2. Cut out two rectangles to the dimensions given and drill the screw holes as shown in diagram 2. Remember that the countersinking must be on opposite surfaces, as these two boards will form the left- and right-hand sides of the stove.

DIAGRAM 2

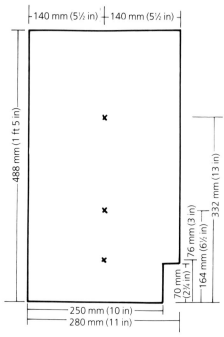

3. On the inside surfaces (that is, those without the countersinking), draw three lines parallel to the bottom and respectively 82 mm (3¼ in), 170 mm (6¾ in) and 338 mm (13½ in) from the bottom. If this has been completed correctly, each of the holes should be 6 mm (¼ in) below a line.

Shelves and base

4. Cut out three simple rectangles, each 326 mm x 256 mm (13 in x 10 in).

Top

5. Cut a 350 mm x 268 mm (13¾ in x 10½ in) rectangle and drill holes as shown in diagram 3. Using a router, or a rasp and sandpaper, round off the three sides marked side A, B, and C on the diagram.

DIAGRAM 3

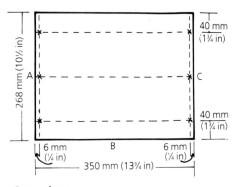

Oven door

6. Cut a 350 mm x 315 mm (13¾ in x 12¼ in) rectangle. Measure in 50 mm (2 in) from each edge and draw a line parallel to the edge to create the outline of the window. Using a jig saw or keyhole saw, cut out the centre section (hatched in on diagram 4a).

7. You will need to drill a lead hole that should be a few centimetres wider than your saw blade on the scrap side of each line. These lead holes are indicated by black dots on diagram 4a.

DIAGRAM 4a

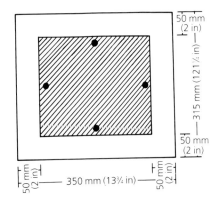

8. Using a router, or a rasp and sandpaper, round off the four outside edges of the door, as well as the four inside edges that will surround the window, on one side of the door only.

Accommodating the window

9. If you have a router, follow these instructions for fitting the window: on the other side (inside) of the door, using a marking gauge set at 15 mm (⅝ in), mark a line around the window space; pencil this line in and extend it to complete the square (dotted line on diagram 4b). Rout out this recess to a depth of 5 mm (¼ in).

DIAGRAM 4b

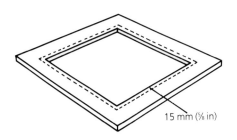

10. If you don't have a router, you have two options for fitting the window: either cut the recess by hand, or set the window straight on to the inside of the door, without any recess.

To cut the recess by hand, draw the squared line around the inside of the door, using a pencil and a marking gauge, as described above.

11. Set your marking gauge at 5 mm (¼ in) and mark a line around the inside edge of the door space (diagram 4b).

12. Cut the dotted line down vertically to a depth of 5 mm (¼ in) with a tenon saw. Before doing so, it will be helpful to clamp a guide piece of wood along the line you intend to cut. This will keep your cut on the line and prevent the saw from wandering. Cut one line at a time, setting up the guide each time before cutting.

13. Using a broad chisel (about 40 mm [1¾ in] wide if possible), gently tap away the scrap, using the 5 mm (¼ in) gauge line as the depth guide, to complete the recess.

14. To set the window into the door without a recess, follow the instructions above for marking a line around the window space (this will act as a guide for securing the window), but don't do any cutting. Because the window will now be above the surface of the door, you will have to take 5 mm (¼ in) off the centre shelf so that the door will close.

Instrument panel

15. Cut a 350 mm x 70 mm (13¾ in x 2¾ in) rectangle from the board; drill four 4mm (⅛ in) holes at the crosses (diagram 5a).

16. Measure in 6 mm (¼ in) from the top edge of the rectangle, and draw a line down the length. At each end, draw in the angle, as shown in diagram 5b. Plane away the scrap wood, which has been hatched in on diagram 5b. Countersink the holes on the sloping side. Round off the edges slightly with sandpaper.

DIAGRAM 5b

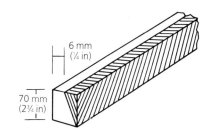

Top trim

17. Cut a rectangle measuring 370 mm x 30 mm (14½ in x 1¼ in). Drill and countersink the holes, as indicated on diagram 6. Using a router, or a rasp and sandpaper, round off both the top and bottom edges of the sides marked A, B and C.

DIAGRAM 5a

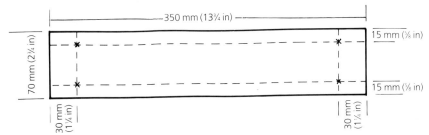

DIAGRAM 6

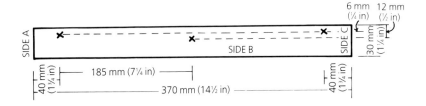

DIAGRAM 7

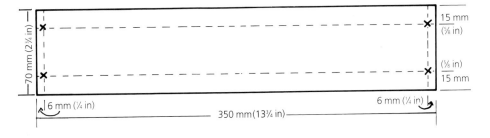

Kick plate

18. Cut a 350 mm x 70 mm (13¾ in x 2¾ in) strip and drill and countersink the holes, as indicated on diagram 7.

Hotplates

19. On the plywood, draw two circles using a compass set at a radius of 60 mm (2½ in) and one of radius 50 mm (2 in). Cut out these circles using a band saw, jig saw or coping saw. Smooth off the edges of each disc, on one side only. This side will be the top.

Drawer front

20. For the drawer front, cut a 350 mm x 105 mm (13¾ in x 4 in) rectangle and drill and countersink the holes (diagram 8).

21. On the opposite side to the countersinking, using a marking gauge set at 10 mm (⅜ in), make a mark along the full length. Pencil this mark in. Using a circular saw, cut a groove above this line. This groove should be the same width as the thickness of the plywood you will use for the drawer base. This is usually the same thickness as most circular saw blades, but it's worth checking before cutting. The depth of this groove should be 5 mm (¼ in) (diagram 9c).

Drawer sides

22. Cut two rectangles each 250 mm x 100 mm (10 in x 4 in) and drill two holes (diagram 9a); do not countersink them yet.

DIAGRAM 8

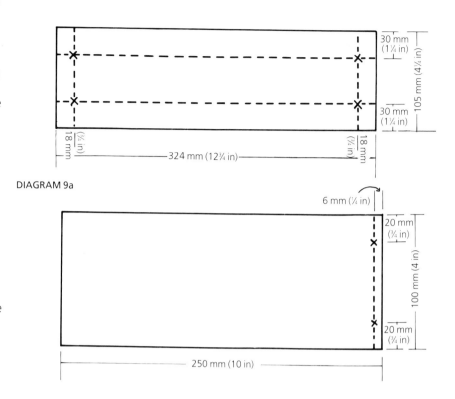

DIAGRAM 9a

DIAGRAM 9b

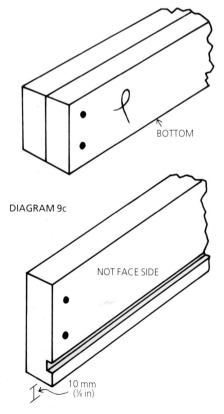

DIAGRAM 9c

23. Hold the two sides together with the screw holes facing, and mark the face side on the outside surface of each piece, pointing downwards (diagram 9b). Set your marking gauge to 10 mm (⅜ in), and draw a line at the bottom of what will be the inside surface (the side opposite the face side). Using a circular saw, cut a groove above this line, along the full length of each piece. This groove should be the thickness of the plywood that you will use for the drawer bottom. This is usually about the thickness of most circular saw blades, but it's worth checking (diagram 9c).

Drawer back

24. Cut one 300 mm x 80 mm (12 in x 3¼ in) rectangle from the MDF board.

Drawer base

25. Cut a rectangle 312 mm x 255 mm (12¼ in x 10 in) from the plywood.

Stack the five drawer sections together and set aside for later.

Construction

As we now have all the major components of the stove, we can begin the construction process. It is a good idea to first construct the stove without using any glue. This way, you will be able to ensure that all the components are the right size and that everything fits together well. If any adjustments need to be

made, they can be made at this stage. (Diagrams 10a & 10b provide useful guidelines as to the general layout of the pieces.)

When constructing the stove, remember that for each screw there must be a lead hole in the receiving piece of wood. This lead hole should be the same width as the shank of the screw and the same depth as the amount the screw will protrude from the first piece of wood.

DIAGRAM 10a

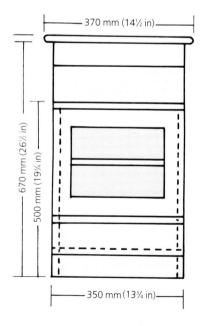

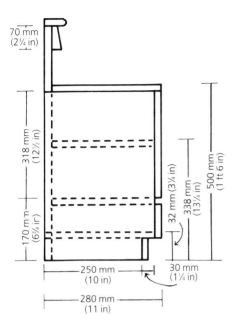

70 mm (2¾ in)
318 mm (12½ in)
170 mm (6¾ in)
500 mm (1 ft 6 in)
338 mm (13¼ in)
32 mm (3¼ in)
250 mm (10 in)
30 mm (1¼ in)
280 mm (11 in)

Fitting the sides
26. Place the stove back on a flat work surface (with the countersinkings against the surface) and clamp it with a G-clamp at each end. Take one of the side pieces and hold it in position against the back, making sure that the countersinkings on this piece lie towards you. Drill one lead hole and screw the side into place — this should hold it in an upright position. Drill the remaining lead holes and screw into place.

27. Unclamp the back and spin it around so that it is in position for the other side piece to be fitted. Reclamp it to the work surface to hold it firmly in place. Repeat the instructions above to fit the other side piece.

Fitting the shelves
28. Leaving the work in position, collect the pieces that form the base and shelves. Take one piece and place it into position inside the stove so that the top surface edge is flush with one of the internal pencil lines. Use a square to check that it is at right angles to the back before drilling one lead hole and screwing it in place. Check that it is still at right angles to the base, then drill the remaining holes and screw into place.

29. Repeat these instructions to fix the other two pieces to the side facing you.

30. Spin the back around and secure the loose ends of these three pieces in position.

Fitting the top
31. Stand the stove upright and put the top in place. It should fit flush against the back

of the stove, while at the same time being flush with the sides and the front edges of the sides. When you're satisfied that it fits well, hold it in place and drill the two lead holes closest to the back board. Screw into position. Drill the remaining lead holes and set in the appropriate screws.

Fitting the kick plate
32. Lay the stove on its back and hold the kick plate in position. Check and fit as you have just done for the top.

Fitting the hotplates
33. Draw guidelines on the surface of the top as in diagram 11. Spread a thin layer of glue on the underside of each hotplate and press firmly into place. Leave the top in a horizontal position for the plates to dry.

Fitting the instrument panel
34. Leaving the stove on its back, hold the instrument panel in position, keeping the top flush with the top of the stove and the sides flush with the sides of the stove. Hold in position and drill any one lead hole. Screw this into place. When you're satisfied that it is straight and true, drill the remaining lead holes and screw into place.

Fitting the top trim
35. Stand the stove in an upright position and hold the top trim in position, with the back of the top trim flush with the back of the stove and the ends of the top trim overlapping the sides of the stove by 10 mm (⅜ in) on each side. When you're satisfied that the positioning is correct, hold it in position and drill the lead hole for the

DIAGRAM 11

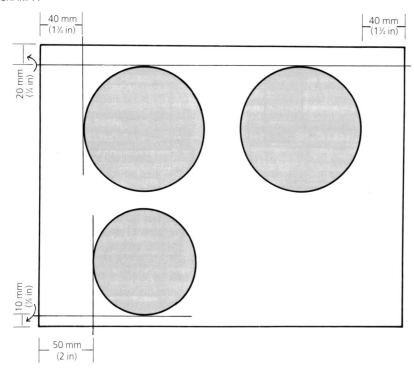

40 mm
(1¾ in)

40 mm
(1¾ in)

20 mm
(¾ in)

10 mm
(⅜ in)

50 mm
(2 in)

centre screw and fix that screw in place. Drill the lead holes for the remaining two holes and screw these into place.

Fitting the door

36. Fit the two hinges, first to the bottom inside surface of the door and then to the shelf, 40 mm (1¾ in) from each end, as shown in diagram 12. Make sure that the butt of each hinge is exactly parallel with the edge of the shelf and door. The Perspex will only be fitted into the door after the door has been painted.

DIAGRAM 12

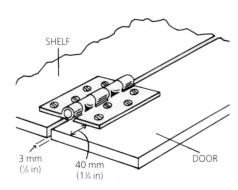

SHELF

3 mm
(⅛ in)

40 mm
(1¾ in)

DOOR

Constructing the drawer

When constructing the drawer, it is important to remember that, in order for the drawer to slide easily, it has to be about 2 mm (1/16 in) clear on each side. If there is any less clearance than this, the drawer will stick; more than this, and the drawer will wobble from side to side as well.

37. Following the same method of fixing as you have already employed on the other sections, fix the two sides to the front. The inside grooves that you cut should form one continuous groove right around the inside of the three sides. Fix the back between the sides, so that the bottom of the back section is flush with the top of the groove. Diagram 13 shows you how the drawer should look at this point.

DIAGRAM 13

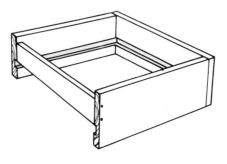

38. Slide the plywood bottom into position. In order to achieve a good fit it may be necessary to taper the sides using a plane. Do not cut them shorter! Plane until a good fit is achieved. The tapering should be on the underside of the drawer. The drawer should now slide into the drawer space, fit well and slide in and out easily.

Finishing

39. If you are satisfied that the whole stove is as it should be, it can now be taken to pieces. Sand all edges smooth and repeat

the whole construction procedure, this time using a thin layer of wood glue on each surface to be joined. You will need to secure the base of the drawer with three or four evenly spaced panel pins at the back on the underside as well as a little glue. Do not fit the drawer, the door, the Perspex in the door, or the door handles until after you have completed the painting.

Painting

40. Use wood filler to fill screw holes and any unsightly gaps. When the filler is thoroughly dry, sand it down until flush with the surrounding surfaces.

41. Apply a coat of undercoat to the stove, the door, and the front and the edges of the front of the drawer (do not paint the inside of the drawer space).

42. When the paint is thoroughly dry, give it a good sanding down and then apply the topcoat of your choice, being careful to paint neatly around the hotplates.

43. Give the hotplates a coat of matt black, which is more realistic than a gloss paint. You may find it necessary to apply two topcoats for a really good finish.

Final construction

44. When all the paint is thoroughly dry, screw the Perspex window into place on the inside of the door, using two small screws on each edge.

45. Fit the door into place.

46. Secure one end of the length of chain inside the oven, 50 mm (2 in) from the top and 20 mm (¾ in) from the edge, using two small screws. Support the open door so that it is at right angles to the stove and fix the other end of the chain to the inside of the door at a convenient point. When the door is opened, it should be supported at 90° to the stove. For added strength it is a good idea to attach a second chain, on the other side of the door. Fit the magnetic door catch into place in one corner of the oven and door.

47. Drill a hole in the centre of each bottle top and screw it into position on the instrument panel (the exact position isn't critical). Leave enough 'play' in the fitting to allow the 'dial' to turn realistically.

48. Fit the handles on the oven door and the drawer as shown in the photograph.

49. Give the bottom edges and the sides of the drawer a light rubbing with candle wax to ensure that it slides easily into place.

FURTHER READING

Woodworking techniques

Atkinson, Scott (editor) *Basic Woodworking*, Sunset Publishing, California, 1991.

Blizzard, Richard *Blizzard's Book of Woodworking*, Betterway Publications, Ohio, 1991.

Engler, Nick *The Workshop Companion: Joining Wood*, Rodale Press, Emmaus, Pennsylvania, 1992.

Hasluck, Paul J *The Handyman's Book*, Ten Speed Press, Berkley, California, 1987.

Jones, Bernard *The Complete Woodworker*, Ten Speed Press, Berkley, California; *The Practical Woodworker*, Ten Speed Press, Berkley, California.

London College of Furniture *The Woodworker's Handbook*, Penguin Group, London, 1992.

Masterson, Alf *The Woodworker's Bible*, A & C Black, London, 1990.

Newland, James *The Carpenter's Assistant*, Bracken Books, London, 1992.

Scott, Ernest *The Mitchell Beasley Illustrated Encyclopedia of Working in Wood*, Mitchell Beasley Publishing Ltd, London, 1992.

Wearing, Robert *The Resourceful Woodworker* B T Batsford Ltd, London, 1991.

Woodworking Projects

Conran, Terence *Toys and Children's Furniture*, Conrad Octopus Ltd, London, 1992.

Forde, Terry *Easy-to-Make Wooden Toys*, David and Charles, Great Britain, 1991; *Fun-to-Make Wooden Toys*, David and Charles, Great Britain, 1991.

Jenkinson, David *Wheel-it, Ride-it Wooden Toys*, David and Charles, Great Britain, 1992.